MIRACLE POWER
for
INFINITE RICHES

Joseph Murphy, D.D., Ph.D, LL.D.
Fellow of the Andhra Research University, India

Parker Publishing Company, Inc.
West Nyack, New York

© 1972 *by*

Parker Publishing Company, Inc.
West Nyack, New York

20   19

Reward Edition . . . . . June, 1974

Other books by the author:

Amazing Laws of Cosmic Mind Power
The Cosmic Power Within You
Infinite Power for Richer Living
Miracle of Mind Dynamics
The Power of Your Subconscious Mind
Secrets of the I Ching
Your Infinite Power to Be Rich
Psychic Perception: The Magic of Extrasensory Power

Library of Congress Cataloging in Publication Data

Murphy, Joseph,   (date)
    Miracle power for infinite riches.

    1. Success. I. Title.
BJ1611.M87   110   72-6594
ISBN 0-13-585638-8

PRINTED IN THE UNITED STATES OF AMERICA

How This Book Can Bring Riches to You

Have you ever asked yourself these questions?

— Why is one man very rich and the other poor?

— Why does one man succeed in business while another fails in the same business?

— Why is it that one man prays for wealth and gets no answer and another member of his family prays and gets immediate results?

— Why is it that one man uses affirmations for money and success and becomes poorer and another man uses the same affirmations and gets marvelous results?

— Why is it that one man is trying to sell his home or property for a year or more with no success and his neighbor sells his home and property in a few days?

— Why does one man become a great success as a salesman in a particular territory and another man in the same territory becomes a failure?

— Why is it one man goes up the ladder in his profession while another man with equal credentials toils and

moils all his life without achieving anything worth-
while?

— Why is it that one man has all the money he needs to
accomplish his objectives and the other man can't
make ends meet?

— Why is it that so many religious, good, kind people
are always short of money and other religious people
have all the money they need and use it wisely?

— Why is it that so many atheistic, agnostic and irre-
ligious people succeed, prosper, become immensely
wealthy and enjoy radiant health while at the same
time many good, kind, moral, upright religious people
suffer sickness, lack, misery and poverty?

— Why is it that some give and never receive in return
and others give and they receive bountifully?

— Why does one man have a beautiful, luxurious home
while another lives in the slums or a dilapidated
home?

— Why is it that the rich get richer and the poor get
poorer?

— Why is it that one sister is happily married and leads
a rich life and the other sister is lonesome and
frustrated?

— Why is it that one man's belief makes him rich and
the other man's belief makes him poor, sick and a
failure in life?

This book answers all the foregoing questions and is
intensely practical and down-to-earth. It is intended for men
and women who wish to experience the riches which are all
around them. You are here to lead a full and happy life and
have all the money you need to do whatever you want to do
and when you want to do it. *Money should be circulating
freely in your life and there should always be a surplus of
it for you.*

You can get immediate results by using the laws of
your mind in the right way. There are simple, practical
techniques and easy-to-do programs in every chapter of this

book, enabling you to put into practice at once the art of living life gloriously, richly and abundantly. You will find detailed instructions as to how to become rich. You will find many examples of men and women in this book who were penniless, and down and out, and yet who learned to tap the treasure house of their subconscious mind and found their true place in life, thereby attracting all the riches they needed to lead a full, happy and prosperous life.

In writing the many chapters of this book, I had in mind the salesman, the busboy, the housewife, the stenographer, the businessman, the clerk behind the counter, the professional man, the student, the intern in the hospital and all those who need money and want money to fulfill their dreams, aspirations and ambitions in life. Therefore, you will find each chapter pregnant with numerous, simple and intensely practical techniques, the what-to-do, and how-to-do-it, for impregnating your subconscious mind, knowing that whenever you impress the idea of wealth the right way in your subconscious, you will experience riches waiting for you on the screen of cosmic space. It is that simple to become wealthy!

All of the many case histories outlined in this book are of men and women in this country and also in other lands across the sea (as my books are published in many foreign languages) who became immensely wealthy and successful by using the mental and spiritual laws described in detail. I might add, these men and women "belonged" to religions of all known kinds, and some were definitely atheists and agnostics who had no religious affiliations of any kind! Yet, by applying the impersonal powerful forces outlined in this book, they prospered in a magnificent way and became transformed men and women, and enjoyed their wealth for true richer living.

As far as I know, these people, in their writings and personal conversations, came from every income bracket, including many who were bankrupt and penniless and from every social level. All of these men and women have amassed wealth and have achieved their desired goals in life by using the powers of their subconscious mind in the right way. They are always destined thereby to go forth conquering every obstacle to acquiring unlimited wealth.

Unique Features of This Book

You will be amazed at this book's down-to-earth practicality. You are presented with simple, usable formulas and techniques which anyone can apply in the workaday world. The special features of this book will enlighten, appeal and reveal to you the reason why oftentimes many people get the opposite of what they prayed for. This book will also point out to you clearly the reasons why.

The age-old cry which you yourself have often heard is, "Why is it I prayed and prayed and yet I receive no answer?" In this book you will find the simple answer to this common complaint. The many simple programs, formulas and techniques for impregnating your subconscious mind and getting the *right answers* make this an extraordinarily valuable book in extracting from the treasure house of eternity within you all the riches you need — spiritual, mental, material and financial — enabling you to lead a full, happy, rich and joyous life. *God gave you richly all things to enjoy* (I Timothy 6:17).

Some Highlights of This Book

The following are just some of the many highlights of this book:

- How an engineer in a deep financial jam broke the fixation spell, and at the end of a few days was advanced $25,000, which solved his problems (page 28).
- How a daughter revealed the riches of the Infinite Healing Presence to her mother by giving her a transfusion of faith and confidence, bringing about a wonderful restoration of her mind and body (page 28).
- How a young lady broker became a marvelous suc-

cess by maintaining a mental picture of success and riches (page 30).

— How a young banker quiets his mind and receives marvelous financial answers from his subconscious for himself and his customers (page 31).

— The reason why some do not get answers from their subconscious and how to overcome this (pages 67-69).

— How a psychologist about to lose everything in a lawsuit received everything bequeathed to her by directing her subconscious the right way (page 33).

— How a young secretary drew up a treasure map and received out of the blue $50,000, a trip around the world, married a wonderful man and now has a beautiful home magnificently furnished (page 96).

— How a widow trying unsuccessfully to sell a home for over a year, by following instructions in this book, within three days received $100,000 for the home, which was the full price she wanted (page 97).

— How an unemployed actress suddenly became a motion picture actress by using mental imagery as well as acquiring an outstanding, wealthy man for a husband (page 100).

— How a man followed the instructions of using the Master Image and discovered an oil well, has obtained a beautiful mansion, four cars, and in three months' time has become worth a half million dollars. It is written, "Whoever perseveres will be crowned" (page 102).

— How a salesman with dim prospects for the future was made sales manager at $30,000 plus fringe benefits. He practiced the technique of thought-image in this book (pages 83-84).

— How a young Spanish girl used one of the techniques in this book and found $2,000 in an envelope on the street, enabling her to take her mother on a trip to Mexico (page 85).

There is a simple, practical, logical and scientific way that always works for you to have all the good things of life, plus all the money you need for yourself and your family. I want to say positively, definitely, unquestionably and decisively that by using the instructions in this book, you will reap the fruits of a rich, happy and successful life that you want for yourself.

Let this book guide you. Go over it again and again, do exactly as it says, and you will open the door to fabulous riches waiting for you, plus a nobler, finer and satisfying life. From this page onward, let us go forward in the light of true workable knowledge till the day you have been expecting breaks, and all the shadows of fear, failures you may have been experiencing, flee away suddenly. Then miracle of miracles, you *are* the wealthy person you have always wanted to be.

Joseph Murphy

Contents

How to Start Living Like a King —
Almost Overnight (continued)................... **210**

one

The Secret of
Miracle Power for
Infinite Riches

It is your God-given birthright to be rich, which means you are here to express the fullness of life along all lines for glorious living. You exist on earth to lead a happy, joyous and glorious life; in other words, the life more abundant. Infinite riches are omnipresent, and you should begin to realize that the treasure house of infinity is within your own subconscious depths. Begin now to extract from that marvelous gold mine within you everything you need — money, friends, a lovely home, beauty, companionship and all the blessings of life. Whatever you want, you can bring forth when you apply the proper technique, i.e., when you apply the "know-how" of accomplishment.

Dave Howe, an old friend of mine, told me about two geologists who had graduated from the same college and who had been brought up in the same town. One knew about the mind's treasure house within him; the other did not, but he depended on externals such as physical appearances, conditions and general topography of the soil. This man spent three weeks in a certain area in Utah with all the modern equipment of his profession and found nothing. The other man with the right mental equipment followed up in the same area and found in the first hour a vein of uranium and a vein of silver.

Where was the wealth, the riches? I believe you will conclude that the real riches were within the mind of the second geologist who believed in a guiding principle within his subconscious which would lead him straight to the hidden wealth.

The Greatest Secret in All the World

One man recently said to me that the greatest secret being unfolded today was in the genetic field, and that now as a consequence modern science could alter man's basic genes so that we could create as many Einsteins, Beethovens, Edisons, etc., as we would like. He failed to see that the Living Spirit (God) is within man, which can't be changed; it is the same yesterday, today and forever. Man is more than his body, his hereditary characteristics, his family tree and the color of his skin, eyes and shape of his body.

Man is transformed only one way, and that is by the transformation of his mind. *Be ye transformed by the renewing of your mind* (Romans 12:2). Others say that interplanetary travel and nuclear fission represent the greatest secrets of our times. The greatest secret is that the Kingdom of God is within man, which means that infinite intelligence, boundless wisdom, infinite power, infinite love and the answer to every problem under the sun are locked in his own subconscious mind.

Man is looking for the greatest secret in the world everywhere but within himself. Begin now to tap these tremendous powers within you, and you will begin to lead a full and happy life based on . . . *God, who giveth us richly all things to enjoy* (I Timothy 6:17). *I am come that they might have life, and that they might have it more abundantly* (John 10:10).

Your Right to Be Rich

It is normal and natural for you to desire prosperity, success, achievement and recognition in your life. You should have all the money you need to do what you want to do, and when you want to do it. There is no virtue in poverty because poverty is a mental disease, and it should be abolished from the face of the earth. Wealth is a state of mind; likewise, poverty is a state of mind. We will never eradicate all the slums in the world until we first wipe out the slums and belief in poverty and lack in the mind of man.

During private counseling and when talking to people in foreign lands as well as during interviews with people following lectures, both here and abroad, I hear the constant old refrain: "There is nothing that $25,000 or $50,000 would not cure in my life." This refers, of course, to those who suffer from pecuniary embarrassment and who are financially handicapped. They fail to realize that wealth is really a thought-image in the mind, and that if they follow the simple techniques as outlined in this book, in using their subconscious mind, wealth will flow to them in avalanches of abundance.

It is your right and that of your family to have excellent food, good clothes, an ideal home and all the money you need to buy the good things of life. You need a period every day for meditation, prayer, relaxation and recreation, and the time and facilities necessary should be available to you. To prosper means that you begin to advance mentally, spiritually, intellectually, socially, financially and along all lines.

How He Discovered the Riches of His Mind

Recently I talked with a man who said that he had had a streak of bad luck and misfortune. He owned a home, but it was mortgaged to the hilt. He didn't have enough money to buy the basic necessities of life for his family. Also, he could not meet the mortgage payment or the grocery bills.

His medical expenses were being paid by his brother, and, in his own words, his life was a mess.

Tapping the Riches of His Subconscious

I explained to this man how the infinite intelligence within his subconscious could reveal to him everything he needed to know at all times; that he could receive inspiration, guidance, new, creative ideas and a solution to financial problems. I added that if he used his subconscious correctly, it also would provide all the money he needed, and that he could experience financial freedom beyond his fondest dreams.

Accordingly, I gave him two abstract ideas: wealth and success. He agreed that wealth is everywhere and that he was born to succeed and to win in the game of life, as the infinite power within him cannot fail. At my suggestion, he relaxed, became quiet at night and repeated slowly, feelingly and with deep understanding: "Wealth, success; wealth, success," taking these ideas into the deep of sleep. He understood that whatever he impressed on his subconscious would be magnified and multiplied on the screen of space.

The secret is that his last waking concept prior to sleep is etched on his subconscious mind. Each night as he repeated these two words, "wealth, success," he was activating and releasing the latent powers of his subconscious and, the law of his subconscious being compulsive, he was compelled to express riches and success.

How His Subconscious Responded

This man, recognizing that the source of his supply was his own subconscious mind, proved that when used in the right way, it never fails, and in unforeseen ways meets his needs regardless of circumstances. He was offered $25,000 cash for a lot which he had had for ten years, and for which he was in arrears for monthly payments, and which he had been unable to sell for over a year. His lot was needed for a new building, which the purchasers wished to construct at once. He discovered that infinite riches are all around him, as well as within him.

The thought in his mind was the connecting link which united him with the treasure house of infinity. Infinite intelligence within your subconscious can only do *for* you what it can do *through* you. Your thought and feeling control your destiny. I can assure you that this man, as he follows the technique I gave him, will never be wanting all the days of his life.

The Riches of the Listening Ear and Understanding Heart

Recently I had a wonderful letter from a widow who listens every morning to my radio program. The following is the essence of the letter. She pointed out that her husband had died a year previously and had left no insurance. She had three children to support, the house was mortgaged, and she had only $500 in the bank. Friends paid the funeral expenses for her deceased husband. She wrote: "I heard you quote from the Bible: *But my God shall supply all your needs according to his riches in glory* (Philippians 4:19), and you elaborated on this by telling us that if we tune in on the Infinite within us and believe in our hearts that no matter what it is we really need to bless us, comfort us, provide for us or inspire us, the Divine Presence would respond, as it is written: *Before they call, I will answer; and while they are yet speaking, I will hear* (Isaiah 65:24).

"I sat down and began to think of God supplying all my needs and hearing me as I was praying, and a great sense of peace and harmony came over me. About two hours later, in walked my brother-in-law, who said to me that he knew of my predicament and that he also was aware of the spending habits and profligacy of his brother."

He told her he wanted to take care of her and the three small children, assuring her that neither she nor they would ever want for the good things of life. He gave her a $10,000 cashier's check and set up an arrangement with his attorney and accountant to see to it that a weekly sum of money was sent to his sister-in-law for the rest of her life. This was in the form of a trust fund, legally instituted, which took care of the children also.

This widow, recognizing that God supplies all her needs, and that even before she asks, the answer is within her, proved to herself the existence of the inexhaustible reservoir within her.

The Secret of Promotion and Riches Was Within Him

A young attorney who had lost a few cases was despondent, gloomy and full of self-criticism and self-condemnation. He found himself with a lot of financial reverses and was deeply in debt. I explained to him that his thoughts are definitely creative and that conditions, circumstances, events and experiences accurately reflect his habitual thinking and imagery. I pointed out that if his thoughts produced lack and limitation, likewise, thoughts of peace, success, prosperity, right action and abundance, sustained regularly and systematically, would reproduce themselves after their kind, in the same manner as men do not reap grapes from thorns or figs from thistles. For the law is that man is what he thinks all day long.

Moreover, it is true that *one spiritual thought is more powerful than 10,000 negative thoughts,* and that thoughts you originate feelingly and knowingly will create for you whatever you wish to experience from this day forward.

I laid out a program for him to follow and asked him to remind himself frequently of the riches of the infinite within his subconscious mind. Accordingly, I gave him the following prayer technique. He affirmed slowly, quietly and feelingly as follows, three to four times a day:

"Today is God's day. I choose harmony, success, prosperity, abundance, security and Divine right action. Infinite intelligence reveals to me better ways to give greater service.

I am a mental and spiritual magnet, irresistibly attracting to me men and women who are blessed, comforted and satisfied with my counsel and decisions on their behalf. I am Divinely guided all day long, and whatever I do will prosper. Divine justice and Divine law and order govern all my undertakings, and whatever I begin will result in success. I know the law of my mind, and I am fully aware that all these truths I am reiterating are now sinking into my subconscious mind, and they will come forth after their kind. It is wonderful."

He made it a special point never to deny what he affirmed, and when thoughts of lack, fear or self-criticism came to him, he would immediately reverse the thought by affirming: *The Lord is my shepherd. I shall not want* (Psalm 23:1).

A few years have passed by, and today this young man has gone up the ladder of success. He is now a prominent judge. When your thoughts are God's thoughts, God's power is with your thoughts of good.

How a Salesman Hit the Jackpot

A real estate salesman who attends my lectures on Sunday mornings and listens to my radio program, said to me that his sales were falling off badly and that he had incurred a lot of financial obligations and found himself deeply in debt. He added that he had not made a sale of property or a home in eight months.

In talking to him, I discovered that he was envious, jealous and highly critical of the sales techniques and processes of other salesmen who were making almost daily sales. I pointed out to him that jealousy and envy generated by himself would tend to impoverish him and attract all sorts of lack, limitation and misery to him. He was made to see that his thought is definitely creative and that what he thinks and wishes for the other, he will create in his own experience, for the simple reason that he is the only thinker in his universe and is definitely responsible for the way he thinks about others as well as about himself.

He then reversed his attitude of mind and began to wish

sincerely for all his associates success, achievement, wealth and all the blessings of life. His constant prayer is:

"I am a child of the Infinite, and His riches flow to me freely, joyously and endlessly. I am enriched in all ways with happiness, peace, wealth, success and outstanding sales. I am now stirring up the riches of my deeper mind and rich results follow. I know I shall reap what I sow, for it is written: *Thou shalt also decree a thing, and it shall be established unto thee; and the light shall shine upon thy ways* (Job 22:28)."

Today he is a sales manager and is able and capable of instructing others how to sell wisely, judiciously and constructively. The Book of Proverbs says: *Poverty and shame shall be to him that refuseth instruction* (Proverbs 13:18).

MEDITATION FOR REALIZING
THE ABUNDANT LIFE

Repeat the following meditation to help solve your problems for abundant living:

"I know that to prosper means to grow spiritually along all lines. God is prospering me now in mind, body and affairs. God's ideas constantly unfold within me bringing to me health, wealth and perfect Divine expression.

"I thrill inwardly as I feel the Life of God vitalizing every atom of my being. I know that God's Life is animating, sustaining and strengthening me now. I am now expressing a perfect, radiant body full of vitality, energy and power.

"My business or profession is a Divine activity, and since it is God's business, it is successful and prosperous. I imagine and feel an inner wholeness functioning through my body, mind and affairs. I give thanks and rejoice in the abundant life."

CHAPTER POINTS TO REMEMBER

1. You are here to lead the abundant life, a life full of happiness, joy, health and rich living. Begin now to release the riches of the treasure house within you.

2. The real riches are within your subconscious mind. A geologist who believed in the guiding principle of his subconscious mind found the treasure in the earth the first hour; his associate, lacking this faith, had worked in that area for three weeks and had found nothing.

3. The greatest secret in all the world is that God indwells man, but the average man is looking everywhere but within himself for wealth, success, happiness and abundance. God is the Life Principle, the Infinite Intelligence and Infinite Power within man, available instantly to all men through the medium of man's thought.

4. Poverty is a disease of the mind. Belief in poverty and lack produce lack and limitation. Wealth is a state of mind. Believe in the law of riches, and you shall receive. Before we will ultimately banish the slums and poverty, we must first banish the slums and false beliefs in the mind of man.

5. You can tap the riches of your subconscious by claiming guidance, abundance, wealth, security, and right action. Make a habit of meditating on these truths and your subconscious will respond accordingly.

6. If you lull yourself to sleep every night with two ideas, wealth and success, knowing that by repeating them you are activating the latent powers of your deeper mind, you will be compelled to express wealth and success.

7. Infinite intelligence in your subconscious can only do for you what it can do through you. Your thought and feeling control your destiny.

8. When you believe that the nature of the infinite intelligence in your subconscious mind is to respond to the nature of your request, the answers will always come to you and in ways you know not of.

9. Your thoughts are creative. Each thought tends to manifest itself in your life. Thoughts of promotion,

riches, expansion, and achievement, provided you do not deny them subsequently, come forth after their kind. You promote yourself. You answer your own prayer because it is done unto you as you believe.

10. Be careful when you affirm wealth, success, right action and promotion that you do not subsequently deny what you affirm. That would be like mixing an acid with an alkali, and you would get an inert substance. In other words, stop neutralizing your good. Thoughts are things. What you feel you attract and what you imagine you become.

11. Be sure that you are not envious or jealous of the success, riches and wealth of others. Your thought is creative, and if you are envious or critical of those who have amassed wealth and honors, you will impoverish yourself along all lines. *Your thought is creative, and what you think about the other you tend to create in your own experience.*

12. Whatever you really feel to be true and so decree in your life will definitely come to pass. Decree riches, health, beauty, security and right action. *Thou shalt also decree a thing, and it shall be established unto thee; and the light shall shine upon thy ways* (Job 22:28).

13. Use the meditation at the end of the chapter to realize a more abundant life.

two

How to Tap the Miracle Power That Makes You Rich at Once

The Bible says: *If thou canst believe, all things are possible to him that believeth* (Mark 9:23).

To believe is to accept something as true. When you analyze the root of the word, you learn it means to be alive, i.e., make alive the truths of God by feeling the reality of them in your heart. It is much more than a conscious or theoretical assent; it means that you must feel the truth of what you affirm in your heart.

It is belief in the minds of men that determines the difference between success and failure, health and sickness, happiness and unhappiness, joy and sadness, wealth and poverty. Wealth is a state of mind, as poverty is a state of mind. You are truly rich when you are acquainted with the Infinite Presence and Power within you which men call God. You are truly rich when you know that your thought is creative, that what you feel you attract, and that what you imagine you become. You are rich when you know the creative process of your mind, which is that whatever you impress on your subconscious mind will be projected on the screen of space as form, function, experience and events.

How He Discovered the Riches Within

A young engineer said to me, "I am in a big jam and I have been praying continually, getting nowhere." I suggested to him that it wasn't necessary for him to pray continually as if he were afraid to let go, but to leave it to the infinite intelligence of his subconscious mind. I explained to him that he could break the *fixation spell* and discover the spiritual riches within him by praying for someone else — John next door or May down the street, who is known to be up against it with a terrible heart condition, etc. — twice a day. I suggested also that he pray for joy by claiming, "The joy of the Lord is my strength; knowing that joy is the *élan* of life, the expression of life." He was to use no will power or mental coercion in this mental and spiritual approach.

At the end of a few days, a complete solution to his problem came out of the blue. He said to me, "I was about to lose everything, when an old friend came to my aid by advancing me $25,000, which solved all my problems." This man had discovered that riches are in the infinite storehouse of his subconscious mind.

She Discovered the Riches of
Her Creative Thought

A young woman was quite concerned about her mother, who was afflicted with chronic stomach pains. The digestive tablets and antispasmodic medicine which her doctor had prescribed failed to relieve her pains. The daughter was setting aside half an hour in the morning and half an hour every evening praying about her mother's stomach — that the stomach was a Divine idea, that it was perfect, that her digestion was perfect, etc. The unfortunate result was that she got stomach trouble herself.

I explained to her that in order to help her mother, she must refrain from identifying with her mother's stomach ailment and keeping an appointment with it, because by her attitude she was holding on to the trouble by this close association. It had become a habit keeping a date with her mother's stomach pains. She had a sort of contract job.

How Her Creative Thought Healed

She changed her procedure and ceased dwelling upon organs of the body and other corporeal conditions. She identified with the infinite healing presence in the subconscious mind and began to claim quietly, feelingly and lovingly that the healing presence and intelligence in the subconscious, which created her mother's body, was vitalizing, healing, and restoring her whole being into harmony, health, peace and wholeness. She meditated quietly on these truths for a reasonable period of time, feeling that this particular prayer was the best she could do at the time, and then she would pray again when she felt the need to do so. Her results with this approach were remarkable, in that all distress vanished from her mother, and she, herself, was also set free.

Sympathy and Compassion

The reason this woman became ill while praying for her mother was because she was actually sympathizing with her, thereby submerging in the quicksand with the other. Compassion consists of standing on firm ground and throwing a rope or branch of a tree to the other and pulling him out. Sympathy means to agree with the negative or baleful aspects of the condition, which tends to aggravate the problem and which actually magnifies it. The reason for this is that whatever we focus our attention on, the subconscious magnifies exceedingly.

Giving the Riches of the Infinite to the Sick Person

All the riches of the Infinite, such as inspiration, guidance, faith, confidence, joy, harmony, love, peace, abundance and security are within you. Therefore, it behooves you when you visit a sick person to lift him up in your thought and feeling, giving him a transfusion of faith and confidence in the healing power of his subconscious. You can also give him courage and understanding. Remind him that with God all things are possible, and imagine him as being whole, radiant, joyous and free. To feel sorry for the ill person and to commiserate with him is to drag him down, and this is a very negative approach. Be compassionate and call forth the infinite healing presence in his subconscious which will heal, bless and restore his mind and body. *He restoreth my soul* (Psalm 23:3).

You Are the Master of Your Thoughts — Not the Servant

Your thought is creative. Every thought tends to manifest itself and causes your subconscious mind to respond according to the nature of your thought. You can direct and steer your thoughts like you steer your automobile. Thoughts are things. Your thought-image of a radio, television, automobile, wealth, health, or a trip to Europe is a reality in your mind. If all the autos in the world were destroyed by some holocaust, an engineer could redesign the vehicle based on the thought-image in his mind, and in a short while we again would have millions of cars.

Your thought is the only instrument you can work with, and it pays fabulous dividends to direct your thoughts wisely, constructively and judiciously. Your thought works with mathematical exactitude: for limitation and lack if you think of poverty; and for expansion, growth and prosperity when you think along these lines.

Her Thought Was the Magnet

A young lady, who is a very successful broker, told me that all her success was due to the fact that she maintained a mental picture of success in her work and it was the magnet which attracted to her the clients and conditions which accurately responded to her thought and feeling.

This was her prayer every morning: "I am a mental and spiritual magnet, attracting to me all those people who want what I have to offer. There is a Divine exchange of ideas between us; they are blessed and I am blessed. I decree harmony, abundance, right action and inspiration, and I know my subconscious mind accepts these truths and assumptions."

This real estate broker finds herself Divinely led and directed along all lines. Her subconscious mind is the seat of habit, and as she continues to claim Divine guidance, right action and abundance regularly and systematically, she is under a subconscious compulsion to do, say and act in the right way. This is the meaning of the saying that "thoughts are things."

He Quiets His Mind and Gets Things Done

During a conversation I had with a prominent banker recently, he told me that some years ago, he had been prone to look only at external conditions and had had the tendency to struggle and resist circumstances and attitudes of associates. He realizes now, however, that it is the quiet mind that gets things done. He quiets his body periodically, tells it to be still and relaxed, and it has to obey. When his conscious mind is quiet, calm, peaceful and receptive, the wisdom of his subconscious rises to the surface, and he receives marvelous answers and solutions.

How He Became a Good Executive

It takes a good executive to draw forth the riches of his subconscious mind. A good executive has the mental acumen and sagacity to delegate work; then he keeps his fingers out of the assignment he has asked the other to complete. A poor executive, whether in business, science, art, industry or education, is always meddling with the pie he has asked the other to make.

When you pray, you must be a good executive and learn to delegate authority to your subconscious mind, which knows all and sees all, and will bring it to pass in its own way. When you pray or seek an answer, you turn your request or desire over to your subconscious mind with complete faith and confidence, knowing that whatever is conveyed to the subconscious will come to pass.

You can know if you have really turned your request over by the way you feel, e.g., if you are wondering how, when, where and through what source, or if you are anxious and apprehensive, you do not really trust the wisdom of your subconscious. Cease pestering or nagging your subconscious. When you think of your desire, lightness of touch is important; remind yourself that infinite intelligence is taking care of it in Divine order.

How He Discovered the Riches of His Mind

Recently I had a conversation with an old friend of mine whose doctor had informed him that it was imperative that he give up smoking at once. He had been smoking four packages of cigarettes daily and felt he just couldn't give them up.

I explained to him an age-old truth: "When your desire and imagination are in conflict, your imagination always wins." At my suggestion, he held a session with himself twice a day, wherein he became quiet and receptive, and affirmed and visioned as follows:

"Freedom and peace of mind are mine now. I know that as I believe and affirm these truths, they are sinking down into my subconscious mind, and I will be under compulsion to give up cigarettes, as the law of my subconscious is compulsion. In my imagination I see my doctor before me. He has just finished examining me and is congratulating me on my freedom from the habit and on my perfect health."

He had a few sessions like this every day for about a

week, at which time he got a response from his subconscious, and he found he had no further desire to smoke. He had succeeded in impregnating his deeper mind with his habitual thinking and visioning. His doctor confirmed objectively what he had been thinking and visioning subjectively. This is how he discovered the riches of his subconscious mind.

The Riches of Letting Go and Letting God Help

A psychologist was involved in a difficult lawsuit requiring her frequent attention and court appearances. Her prayer therapy was as follows: "I let go and let Divine wisdom and Divine right action of my subconscious solve it. I loose the matter and let it go." Whenever she had to get in touch with her attorney or others involved, she would silently decree: "The God-Presence within me is all-wise and is taking care of this in Divine order." She said to me, "I am no longer keeping tabs on the God-Presence within as to how, when, where or through what source this will be solved. I let go and let God take care of it."

The sequel to her new attitude of mind was interesting: the foremost antagonist in the lawsuit passed away one night in his sleep, and the others requested an immediate settlement. There was a Divine adjustment, and she was set free from all legal entanglements.

The Future Can Be Wonderful for You

Do not waste your energy and vital substance by thinking about old peeves, grudges and grievances. To do so is like ripping open a grave — all you find is a skeleton. Focus your attention on the good things of life and realize the future will be wonderful because you know your present and harmonious thoughts will germinate and grow, bringing forth wonderful fruit such as health, happiness, abundance and peace of mind.

Liquidate the past and never mentally touch any negative experience or trauma that has happened in the past. Remain faithful to this mental attitude and realize that as you change your present thoughts and keep them changed, you will change your destiny.

She Discovered the Riches of Scientific Prayer

A mother was distraught and highly agitated because her boy of eighteen had run away from home following an argument with his father. He quit college and joined a hippie colony. She was frantic, and her doctor had to prescribe strong sedatives to quiet her mind and body. In talking to her, I pointed out a few simple truths, such as: you do not own your son; he came through you but not by you. Life-Principle is the common progenitor. We are all children of the one Father, or Self-Originating Spirit. Your son is here to grow, to expand, and to overcome difficulties, challenges and problems, thereby enabling him to discover the powers within him and to release his talents to the world. You can't help him by mental excitation, anger and resentment.

At my suggestion, she decided to release him completely — lock, stock and barrel. She decreed as follows: "I loose my son to God completely. He is Divinely guided in all his ways and Divine wisdom anoints his intellect. Divine law and order reign supreme in his life. He is guided to his true place and is expressing himself at his highest level. I loose him and let him go."

She remained faithful to this prayer and daily claimed peace, harmony, joy and Divine love for herself. Some weeks later, her son went back to college, gave up his old haunts, and is doing well now in his scholastic work. He communicates with both his parents, but his mother no longer feels possessive. She has discovered the riches of Divine love and freedom.

This woman ceased thinking from the standpoint of circumstances and conditions; she began to think from that interior standpoint where there are no circumstances, and from whence she was able to decree what conditions should be according to Divine law and order. Then she let the subconscious wisdom take care of it.

How to Think Richly

Think regularly and systematically of Life, illumination, inspiration, harmony, prosperity, happiness, peace and the life more abundant — think these truths rather than this or that condition of them. Trust the operator of your subconscious mind to bring all these ideas you are contemplating into the way best suited for your particular case. This is a wonderful way to enter into the life more abundant.

MEDITATION TO HAVE THE POWER OF FAITH

Use the following meditation to help you secure the power of faith:

"'The prayer of faith shall save the sick and God shall raise him up.' I know that no matter what the negation of yesterday was, my prayer or affirmation of truth will rise triumphantly over it today. I steadfastly behold the joy of the answered prayer. I walk all day long in the Light.

"Today is God's day; it is a glorious day for me, as it is full of peace, harmony and joy. My faith in the good is written in my heart and felt in my inward parts. I am absolutely convinced that there is a Presence and a perfect Law which receives the impress of my desire now and which irresistibly attracts into my experience all the good things my heart desires. I now place all my reliance, faith, and trust in the Power and Presence of God within me; I am at peace.

"I know I am a guest of the Infinite and that God is my Host. I hear the invitation of the Holy One saying, 'Come unto me all ye that labor, and I will give you rest.' I rest in God; all is well."

CHAPTER POINTS TO REMEMBER

1. To believe is to accept something as true. Belief makes the difference between success and failure,

riches and poverty, health and sickness. Believe in the riches of the infinite power within your subconscious and you will experience them.

2. When you are in "a big jam," break the tension by praying sincerely for someone who is very ill or in deep trouble, and suddenly you will find your own problem solved.

3. When praying for a loved one, be sure not to identify with the ailment or any part of the anatomy. Realize that the Infinite Healing Presence is flowing through the loved one as harmony, health, peace and joy. Vision the loved one as radiant and happy. Meditate quietly on these truths and pray again when you feel led to do so. Wonders happen as you pray this way.

4. Sympathy means to go down into the quicksand with the other, and it does not help the ill person. Have compassion and give the sick person a transfusion of faith, confidence and love, knowing that with God all things are possible.

5. Your thought is creative, and every thought tends to manifest itself. You can direct and steer your thoughts in the same way as you steer your automobile. Thoughts are things. Your thought-image of wealth, success, and achievement is the magnet that attracts to you all things that correspond with your thought-image.

6. The quiet mind gets things done. Tell your body to be still, and quiet your mind by thinking of the infinite intelligence of your subconscious, which knows the answer. When your conscious mind is still and your body is relaxed, the wisdom of your subconscious will rise to the surface mind.

7. A good executive knows how to delegate authority. You must be a good executive when using your mind. Turn your request over to your subconscious with faith and confidence, and you will get the ap-

propriate response. You know when you have really turned it over, because you are at peace.

8. You can give up smoking or any bad habit by decreeing freedom and peace of mind, while at the same time imagining a friend or a physician congratulating you on your freedom. As you affirm and vision an antipathy toward tobacco, your subconscious will take over and compel your freedom from the habit.

9. Many have discovered the wisdom of turning an acute domestic problem over to the God-Presence, trusting that Divine wisdom and intelligence will bring about the solution which is best for all. The prayer is: "I let go and let God take over," bringing about the perfect answer.

10. Liquidate the past and never dwell on old grievances or grudges. The future is your present thinking made manifest. Think regularly and systematically of harmony, beauty, love, peace and abundance, and you will have a wonderful future.

11. When a son leaves the home in anger, pray as follows: "I loose him to God completely. He is Divinely guided in all ways, and Divine love takes care of him." Whenever you think of him, bless him silently by knowing "God loves him and cares for him." As you do this, whatever happens will be good.

12. Think of the infinite riches within your subconscious mind. Think of harmony, peace, joy, love, guidance, right action, success — all these are principles of life, and as you think of the life more abundant, you activate the latent powers within you. Your subconscious will compel you to express the abundant life right here and right now. Thoughts are things.

13. Use the meditation to secure the great power of faith for yourself.

three

How the Rich Get Richer — and How You Will Join Them

The Bible says: *God, who giveth us richly all things to enjoy* (I Timothy 6:17). Riches are of your mind. There is a guiding principle within you that can lead you to fulfill the desires of your heart. Wealth is a state of consciousness, a mental attitude, an acceptance of the riches of the Infinite. The whole world was here when you were born. Life was a gift to you. Actually, you are not here just to earn a living, because Life itself was a gift to you. You are here to express life and to release your hidden talents to the world.

When you possess the "know-how" of tapping your subconscious mind, you will never want for any good thing all your life, whether it be health, peace of mind, true expression, companionship or a lovely home and all the money you need to do what you want to do when you want to do it. The key of your subconscious to your infinite power to be rich[1] is your own thought. Your thought is creative! Begin to think regularly and systematically of success, achievement, victory, abundance and the good life. *Thinking makes it so.*

---

[1] See *Your Infinite Power to Be Rich* by Joseph Murphy, Parker Publishing Company, Inc., West Nyack, N.Y., 1966.

She Discovered Her Thought-Image Was Wealth

A few years ago I took an Iberian Tour, visiting many famous places in Spain and Portugal. There were about thirty people on this tour. A woman with whom I chatted at Salamanca, Spain, told me she had always wanted to visit Spain because her ancestors had come from Malaga, which we visited. She did not have the necessary funds, but she had been reading *Your Infinite Power to Be Rich,* and she got all the folders and photographs of the famous shrines and cities we were to visit. Her technique was fascinating, and was as follows.

Every night prior to sleep, she would concentrate on the Hotel Malaga Palacio, a picture of which was on the folder. Then she would imagine she was actually sleeping in that hotel and looking at the beautiful surroundings through the window. She followed this procedure for about five nights. One of the young men in the office casually mentioned that he was also going on that trip, they became interested in each other and became engaged prior to the trip. He paid all her expenses as a prenuptial gift.

This event illustrates the working of your deeper mind. It always magnifies what you deposit in it. This woman not only received a gift of the trip, but, in addition, a proposal of marriage and a $2,000 engagement ring. Your subconscious gives you compound interest, and whatever you deposit in it is magnified and multiplied exceedingly. Her thought-image demonstrated to her where all the riches are.

How He Invoked the Law of Increase

On the Iberian Tour mentioned above, we visited the city of Seville, which personifies the real Spain more than any other community in that country. Over half a million people here share the rich history that included Phoenicians, Romans, Moors — all left their mark here. Its university was founded in 1502, and Seville gave the world two of its greatest painters, Murillo and Velasquez.

While conversing with one of the guides in the hotel, I learned that he had left New York City when he was fourteen and that he had developed an intense desire to go to the city of his ancestors (Seville) to learn languages and to become a guide, travelling through Europe and interpreting for tourists. He invoked the powers of his subconscious in a simple way without conscious knowledge of how it worked. This is the way he worked.

He wrote out on a piece of paper that he wanted to go to Seville to study, and to work there to pay for his training while he learned to speak Spanish, French and German. He would affirm this many times a day. He said the most amazing thing happened on his fifteenth birthday: his aunt, who lived in Boston, wrote to his father (her brother) and asked permission to take him along as a companion to Seville to visit her relatives. When they were in that city for a week or so, she consented to pay all his expenses for university training and upkeep with the permission of his father.

This guide's constant prayer is: *The God of Heaven, He will prosper us* (Nehemiah 2:20). By constantly dwelling on his written requests, he succeeded in writing them in the tablets of his subconscious mind, which responded by bringing it to pass in its own unique way.

How to Follow Your State of Mind

The Lord maketh poor and maketh rich: he bringeth low and lifteth up (I Samuel 2:7). The Lord is the lordly power of your subconscious mind, called the Father within, Who doeth the works. Your Lord is what dominates your thinking. If your dominant conviction is that you are entitled to all the good things of life, such as health, wealth, love, true expression and the abundant life, you will experience accordingly. On the other hand, if you feel that you are destined to be poor and that the good things of life are not for you, you are placing yourself in want, lack, frustration and self-imposed bondage.

Remember, your thought has power; it is creative.

Every thought you initiate tends to manifest itself except as it is neutralized by a more powerful thought of greater intensity. All the men and women who garner more of the world's goods reveal a wealth consciousness and a joyous expectancy of the best. Everything you experience is due to the law of your mind. By dwelling on the idea of increased good, and by nourishing it and sustaining it, man draws more of the riches of life to himself. On the other hand, the man who thinks only of decrease, lack and limitation magnifies his loss. The law of your subconscious is to increase any idea implanted in it. The experience of the negative thinker will attract more and more loss.

Begin to Practice the Law of Increase

Remember, any object to which you give special attention will tend to grow and magnify itself in your life. Attention is the key to life. Think of increase along all lines. Feel you are successful and prosperous, since the feeling of wealth produces wealth. Be sure you wish for all those around you success, happiness and abundance, knowing that as you wish increase of wealth and happiness for others, you are also attracting more of God's riches to yourself. As you radiate abundance and riches to others, they will pick up your thoughts subconsciously and will be benefited by the feeling of riches and abundance emanating from you.

You can silently give to all people you meet the following blessing: "God gave you richly all things to enjoy, and you are prospered beyond your fondest dreams." That simple prayer will work wonders in your life.

How to Use the Law of Increase in Business or Professions

As you quietly, lovingly and feelingly enter into the realization that your thoughts of richness, success, prosperity and health create all those conditions and circumstances on which you focus your attention, you will automatically create all the conditions necessary for your advancement. Moreover, you will find yourself attracting more and more people who will become clients, customers, friends and associates, and who will aid you in the realization of your dreams. You will subconsciously attract to yourself the men and women who are living in the consciousness of God's riches.

A businessman in Beverly Hills mentioned to me a while ago the secret of his tremendous success and great popularity with his customers. Every morning when he opens the store, he decrees: "Everyone who enters here is blessed and prospered, inspired and enriched in all ways." He knows the truth, which is: *Thou shalt also decree a thing, and it shall be established unto thee; and the light shall shine upon thy ways* (Job 22:28).

Why the Rich Man Received the Home
Foreclosed on the Poor Man

Not far from where I live, a man's wife was constantly telling him to cease talking about hard times, loss of money, bankruptcy, etc. However, she said he persisted in picturing bankruptcy and loss of his home by constantly saying, "I can't meet the mortgage, we will lose our home, I know I will be bankrupt, business is bad, things never go right for me," and so on. He constantly talked lack, bankruptcy and hard times, and he experienced the unwanted result. The mortgage company foreclosed on his home and he went bankrupt. A successful and prosperous neighbor bought his home for a very small amount of money from the mortgage company, and the rich man acquired the store which he had vacated and is prospering in a wonderful way.

This is why the rich get richer and the poor get poorer. Job said: *The thing which I greatly feared is come upon me* (Job 3:25). The law of mind is good and very good. A man can't begin to think regularly of loss, lack, bankruptcy and failure and expect to prosper and succeed. The rich man walking in the consciousness of success and prosperity and looking upon wealth somewhat like the air he breathes, acquires the former business and home of the poor man. You can't think evil and reap good, no more so than you can think good and reap evil. The law of your mind is perfect. It also outpictures what is impressed upon it. The poor man, a term which means the man who doesn't know how to operate and release the riches of his mind, can at any time he wishes begin to practice the law of opulence and again attract to himself wealth, success and riches of all kinds.

The Rewards of Being Acquainted with the Law of Opulence

You can get acquainted with the qualities of an orange by tasting it and eating it. You can get acquainted with the riches of your subconscious by applying the law of opulence. A businessman said to me that the source of supply was within him and responded to his faith in the endless resources of the infinite riches of his subconscious mind. Every morning and every night his prayer is: "I am ever grateful for God's riches that are ever active, ever present, unchanging and abundant." This businessman never wants for all the money he needs to operate his enterprise and to open up new branches.

Listen to the Truth and You Will Never Be in Want

Infinite Spirit, the source of all blessings, the world, and all things therein contained is within you. You do not own anything in the universe; God, or Spirit, owns all. You are a steward of the Divine and you are here to use the wealth of the world wisely, judiciously, and constructively, claiming Divine wisdom in your handling of all your earthly possessions. When you go on to the next dimension, you cannot take anything with you but the treasures of wisdom, truth and beauty, which you have planted in your subconscious mind. Your faith, confidence and trust in the goodness of God and in the joy of the Lord which is your strength represent the real riches which you take with you into the fourth dimension of life — these are the treasures of heaven (your mind).

In this three-dimensional plane in which we live, you must realize the whole world is yours to enjoy: the cattle on a thousand hills are yours; the song of the birds is yours; you can enjoy the stars in the heavens, the morning dew, the sunset and the sunrise; you can turn your eyes to the hills, the mountains and the valleys, and you can smell the sweet fragrance of the rose, as well as that of the new-mown hay. All the riches in the soil, in the air and in the sea are yours. There is enough fruit that rots in the tropics to feed all of humanity. Nature is bountiful, lavish, extravagant, and actually wasteful.

It is God's intention and will that you lead a full and happy life. You should live in a beautiful home, surrounded by luxury; you should have beautiful clothes, constantly dressing for God and reminding yourself of the infinite and indescribable beauty, order, symmetry and proportion of the Infinite. You constantly should have all the money you need circulating freely in your life, enabling you to do what you want to do, and when you want to do it. Your children should be brought up in beautiful surroundings and in a lovely, God-like atmosphere. Moreover, they should be taught the endless resources within the depths of their own minds, and being able to tap the riches of their subconscious, they will never want for any good thing.

How to Tap the Endless Source of Supply

Recognize the infinite source within your subconscious, and then invoke the great law of opulence and increase along all lines as follows:

"God is the source of my supply, whether it is energy, vitality, creative ideas, inspiration, love, peace, beauty, right action or wealth that I need. I know it is as easy for the creative powers of my subconscious to become all these things as a blade of grass. I am now appropriating mentally and experiencing buoyant health, harmony, beauty, right action, abundant prosperity and all the riches of my deeper mind. I exude vibrancy and good will to all. I am giving better service every day. God's riches are forever flowing into my experience, and there is always a Divine surplus. All these thoughts are sinking down into my subconscious, and they are now coming forth as abundance, security and peace of mind. It is wonderful."

As you sow in your subconscious, so shall you reap. The Bible says: *The wilderness and the solitary place shall be glad for them; and the desert shall rejoice, and blossom as the rose* (Isaiah 35:1).

DAILY MEDITATION FOR THE RICH LIFE

Repeating the following meditation daily will bring the rich life to you faster and easier:

"'Consider the lilies of the field; they toil not, neither do they spin; yet Solomon in all of his glory was not arrayed as one of these.' I know that God is prospering me in all ways. I am now leading the abundant life, because I believe in a God of abundance. I am supplied with everything that contributes to my beauty, well-being, progress and peace. I am daily experiencing the fruits of the spirit of God within me; I accept my good now; I walk in the light that all good is mine. I am peaceful, poised, serene and calm. I am one with the source of life; all my needs are met at every moment of time and every point of space. I now bring 'all the empty vessels' to the Father within. The fullness of God is made manifest in all the departments of my life. 'All that the Father hath is mine.' I rejoice that this is so."

CHAPTER POINTS TO REMEMBER

1. The rich get richer for the simple reason that the consciousness or awareness of wealth and the expectancy of more and more of God's riches, which are omnipresent, attract more and more wealth, health and opportunities to the person who walks in that state of mind.

2. The thought-image of wealth produces wealth; the thought-image of a journey results in the opportunity to take it. A young girl began to think and image from a hotel in Spain, feeling she was there and sleeping there, and her subconscious opened the way and magnified her impression of the journey, adding an engagement and a diamond ring worth $2,000. Your subconscious always magnifies.

3. A young boy of fourteen wrote down his desires for study in a university in Spain to learn languages, to travel and to become a famous guide and interpreter for tourists. He continued to meditate on what he had written and succeeded in writing his requests on the book of life (his subconscious) within him. His subconscious wisdom acted on the mind of his aunt, fulfilling all his desires.

4. Enter into a consciousness of God's wealth, which is all around you. Live in the joyous expectancy of the best, and by the law of attraction, you will attract the riches of the infinite storehouse in your own subconscious mind. Keep thinking of prosperity, abundance, security and increase along all lines.

5. Whatever you give attention to grows, magnifies, and multiplies in your experience. Keep your attention on whatsoever things are lovely and of good report. Radiate abundance, goodwill and riches to others. They will pick it up subconsciously, and you will attract wonderful people into your life. They will prosper and you will prosper.

6. A rich man walks in the mental attitude that wealth is like the air he breathes, and having that state of mind, he attracts more and more riches of all kinds. The poor man who is constantly picturing and talking of lack, bankruptcy and hard times loses his home and business, and often the rich man next door buys them for a song.

7. You can get acquainted .with the riches of the infinite storehouse within you by reiterating and believing the following prayer: "I am ever grateful for God's riches that are ever active, ever present, unchanging and eternal."

8. God gave you richly all things to enjoy in this universe. Life itself is a gift to you. The whole world was here when you were born. Believe and expect the riches of the Infinite, and invariably the best will come to you. As you practice this simple truth, the desert of your life will rejoice and blossom as the rose.

9. Strengthen your hold for a rich life by repeating the meditation at the end of the chapter.

four

How to Claim Your Right to Infinite Riches Now

During the month of May, a few years ago, I took a trip to Ireland, England and Switzerland, and during my stay in Killarney I visited a relative of mine. I might add that Killarney is one of the world's beauty spots. Poets, artists and writers try to convey in their respective media the magnificent and varied color and form of this wonderland of mountains and lakes. These lakes are surrounded by luxuriant woods of birch, oak and arbutus.

It was here amidst the beauty of the countryside that my relative poured out his tale of woe regarding his daughter. Mary (not her real name) was rapidly losing weight and refused to eat except under pressure from her parents. The local doctor was giving her injections of liver and vitamins and said she was a hopeless case. She had been taken to Dublin to see a psychiatrist but refused to talk to him. Her father was frantic, moreover, he was very critical of her.

I had three interviews with her, and on the third interview I asked her point-blank: "Mary, is it true that you are trying to get even with your father, exerting a sort of revenge, because he prefers your brother to you, or at least shows him more attention?" She blurted out: "Yes, I hate him. He never finds fault with my brother but is always criticizing me, and I'm going to make him feel sorry." I pointed out to her that she was slowly committing suicide, which is completely contrary to her religious beliefs; moreover, that her body is a temple of the living God, and that she is here to lead a full, happy and rich life. I added that she would have bodies to infinity, and that by destroying this body, she would solve no problem and would probably be earthbound for a long time, walking about in a dazed and confused condition.

This explanation startled her, and she began to cry and abuse her father with vitriolic language and a flood of tears.

Her Father Came to the Rescue

In his presence, I discussed the matter of his daughter, and he broke down and cried, admitting that he had wanted a boy and had never showed her any affection or love. Her mother had died at her birth. He apologized to his daughter, asked forgiveness, and vowed his love, appreciation and tenderness for her. Actually, this girl was seeking love. She desired to be wanted, loved, cared for and needed. When he exuded and affirmed real love for his daughter, he really poured forth the riches of the Infinite, which is real love.

Mary had been silently saying to herself: "I feel I must starve and die. Nobody loves me. This way I will make my father care for me." But now, with the changed attitude of her father, she wept copiously and began to eat a hearty lunch.

Love frees; it gives; it is the spirit of God. Love opens prison doors, sets free the captives and all those bound by fear, resentment, hostility, etc.

The Prayer That Changed Her Life

"I know my body is the temple where God dwells. I honor and exalt the Divine Presence within me. Divine love fills my soul, and His river of peace flows through my mind and heart at all times. I eat my food with joy, knowing that it is transmuted into beauty, harmony, wholeness and perfection. I know God hath need of me where I am, and I am Divinely expressed. I am loved, I am needed, I am wanted and appreciated by my father and others. I radiate love, peace and goodwill to everyone at all times. My food and drink are God's ideas which unfold within me, making me strong, wholesome and full of Divine energy."

Mary is now saturating her subconscious mind with these truths several times daily. The last letter from her informed me that she is getting married to a very rich local farmer and is bubbling over with a new life and inner joy. She has truly experienced the riches of the Infinite as love, marriage, inner peace and abundance.

The Riches of Faith in a Higher Power

I requested my Irish driver during this European trip to which I referred previously to take me to Glendalough, "The Glen of Two Lakes," which is famous for its historical and archaeological associations. Here in the sixth century, St. Kevin founded a monastery, and his shrine is visited by many people hoping for a cure of various diseases.

My driver told me that as far back as he could remember, he had stuttered badly and was made fun of in school and nicknamed "Stutts." He had been taken to Dublin and Cork City to speech therapists and psychologists to no avail. In desperation, he said, his father had taken him to Glendalough and placed him in the cell in which it was believed St. Kevin had slept. His father had told him, "If you sleep there for an hour, you will be healed."

The driver said, "I believed my father and followed his instructions. When I awakened from the hour's sleep, I was healed, and from that day (twenty years ago), I have never stammered or stuttered in my speech."

The Real Reason for His Cure

I did not disturb this young man's blind faith, which simply activated and released 'the healing power of his subconscious mind. This boy's mind at the age of eight or nine was highly impressionable. His imagination was fired, and his expectancy was undoubtedly 100 per cent belief that St. Kevin would intercede for him. It was done unto him as he believed.

There is only one healing power, and that is the infinite healing presence lodged in your subconscious mind.

The Riches of True Faith Versus Blind Faith

True faith consists in knowing that the Infinite Presence which created you from a cell knows all the processes and functions of your body and certainly knows how to heal you. When you consciously tune in on the healing power of your subconscious, knowing and believing it will respond to you, you will get results. In other words, true faith is the combined use of your conscious and subconscious mind scientifically directed for a specific purpose.

Blind faith consists of belief in amulets, charms, talismans, bones of saints, certain shrines and waters to heal, etc. In other words, it is faith without any understanding and is often only temporary in its therapeutic value.

I suggest to people who are sick to make use of the services of a physician and to keep on praying not only for themselves but also for the physician.

The following are the reasons why:

Honour a physician with the honour due unto him for the uses which ye may have of him; for the Lord hath created him. For of the most High cometh healing, and he shall receive honour of the king.... The Lord hath created medicines out of the earth; and he that is wise will not abhor them... And he hath given men skill, that he might be honoured in his marvellous works.

"My son, in thy sickness be not negligent, but pray unto the Lord, and he will make thee whole... Then give place to the physician, for the Lord hath created him; let him not go from thee, for thou hast need of him. There is a time when in their hands there is good success. For they shall also pray unto the Lord, that he

*would prosper that which they give for ease and remedy
to prolong life . . . "* Ecclesiasticus, Chapter 38: Para-
graphs 1 and 2).

When you pray for health, then health should "spring
forth speedily." If not, you should take action immediately
by going to your medical doctor, dentist, chiropractor, or
surgeon, as seems most appropriate to you. Remember, if
you were always walking in the consciousness of God's love
and peace, you would never be ill. If you can't grow teeth
I suggest you go immediately to a dentist and pray that God
is guiding him, and that Divine law and order reigns supreme
in your life, and you will be satisfied with your new dentures.

Why He Did Not Experience the Healing Riches of the Infinite

A friend of mine in Waterford arranged a tour for me
of the Waterford glass factory, the glass of which is legen-
dary in its fame. I witnessed experienced craftsmen making
the crystal, the raw material of Waterford glass blooming
into depth and sparkle. One of the craftsmen caused a ray
of light to fall on the cut crystal; then the real glory of its
facets, diamonds, flutings and ovals shone forth in a spectrum
of indescribable beauty.

But the point I want to make is that my friend was lame
and carried a cane, and he walked with great difficulty. I
asked him whether he was getting medical treatment or not.
He said yes, that cortisone was administered to him and he
took pain pills. Then he asked, "Why is it that when I went to
Scotland and hundreds of people were present at the church
healing meeting which I attended, some cripples threw away
their crutches, others said they could hear for the first time,
and when the healer touched me I felt a strong vibration all
through my body and for the first time I walked without pain
or a cane, but the next day I was as lame and as bad as ever?"

He Had a Temporary Emotional Healing

I explained to him that when the so-called "healer"
placed his hands upon him, manipulating his leg and calling

on Jesus to heal him, at the same time telling him that he was healed and could walk, and in the glare of the lights, the chanting of music and the mass emotional hysteria at the meeting, undoubtedly the emotions aroused from his subconscious depths gave him the power to walk temporarily without the aid of his cane. At the same time the mesmeric or hypnotic suggestions freed him from pain for twenty-four hours. Hypnotic suggestions to the subconscious have only temporary effects. That is what he had experienced.

On the Road to Recovery

My friend began to see that he had not reached the cause of his condition. He began to understand that true, permanent healing comes with forgiveness, love and goodwill to all, and spiritual insight — all these are real healing forces. He admitted he was seething with hostility, guilt, resentment and hatred toward many people. He began to realize that his destructive emotions contributed to his condition. I suggested that he cooperate with his doctor and pray for him and also bless him, which he promised to do.

The Prayer That Is Helping My Arthritic Friend

The following is the prayer I wrote out for him:

"I forgive myself for harboring negative, destructive thoughts about myself and others. I fully and freely forgive everyone, and I sincerely wish for them health, happiness, peace and all the blessings of life. Whenever the person comes into my mind whom I dislike, I will immediately affirm, 'I have released you. God be with you.' I know when I have forgiven others, because 1 feel no sting in my mind. The Infinite Healing Presence of God flows through me, and His river of peace flows through me. I know that Divine love saturates my entire being, and God's love dissolves everything unlike itself. The Healing Light of God is focused at that point in my mind where the problem is and it is shattered, making way for the Holy Spirit (spirit of wholeness) to indwell every thought and every cell. I give thanks for the healing that is taking place now, for I know all healing is of the Most High. I know God is guiding my doctor, and whatever he does will bless me."

He has been reiterating these truths slowly, quietly, and feelingly morning and night, knowing all the while that these spiritual vibrations will enter into his subconscious mind, obliterating the negative patterns lodged there by years of vicious and destructive thinking. The second letter I have received from him said that his local physician is amazed at his progress, and that the calcareous deposits, inflammation and edema are gradually diminishing. He is well on the road to a real spiritual healing, for all healing is of the Most High. *I am the Lord that healeth thee* (Exodus 15:26).

How the Riches of Belief Pay Dividends in All Phases of Life

Blarney Castle is situated five miles from Cork City and is famous for its stone, which has the traditional power of conferring eloquence on all who kiss it. The word "blarney" means pleasant talk, intended to deceive without offending. To kiss the stone, which is set in the wall, one has to lean backwards (grasping an iron railing), and after that kiss the fortunate person is supposed to develop marvelous powers of speech.

I was told by a clergyman visiting here that whereas formerly his sermons had been dull and uninviting, he had become a powerful orator and that after kissing the stone, people flocked to his sermons so that his church was always crowded whenever he gave sermons at mass. This demonstrates the power of belief. The Bible says: *All things are possible to him that believeth* (Mark 9:23).

You will agree that there is no power in a stone to confer the gift of oratory or eloquence, but the belief and expectancy of man stirs up the dormant powers in the depths of the subconscious mind which were always there, waiting to be recognized and utilized. *Wherefore, I put thee in remembrance that thou stir up the gift of God, which is in thee* (II Timothy 1:6).

The Instant Riches of Mental Insight and Understanding·

A man we will call "Johnny" accompanied me on a trip to the Gap of Dunloe in Killarney. Riding through this gap on the sturdy ponies of Kerry is a thrill enjoyed by visitors. In the Ice Age, glaciers carved the mountain out of the surrounding hills. The towering summits of the Reeks, the changing shadows on the mountain tops, and the silence and solitude of the cliff-bound road combine to make an unforgettable impression on the visitor. It was here that my companion got an acute attack of asthma. He used a throat spray, which gave him some relief. He also gave himself a subcutaneous injection of adrenalin.

He said he got an attack about noon every day. Since the attack was sometimes greater than others, a doctor showed him how to use the hypodermic needle in case of emergency. After his attack had subsided, he blurted out, "No wonder I get asthma. My father had it all his life, and I was present when he died from an attack." He was blaming heredity, while at the same time he informed me that he was an adopted son, which of course ruled out his claim of heredity.

How His Mental and Emotional Disturbance Was Released

During a heart-to-heart talk, he admitted that he had hated his foster father ever since the man had told him for the first time, possibly in a fit of anger, "You are not my real son. I took you out of the gutter and gave you a home. You are an illegitimate child." This was a terrible shock to Johnny. He felt guilty because of his hatred and resentment. Though frequently confessing this error, nevertheless it remained suppressed in the deeper recesses of his mind. Being a negative and destructive emotion, it had to have an outlet sooner or later. Then, when his foster father died, he took on the symptoms as a form of self-punishment for his sins.

I explained to him fully the workings of his deeper mind

and pointed out to him that though he undoubtedly deeply resented the fact that he was born out of wedlock, there is no such thing as an illegitimate child in the eyes of God. The real illegitimate child is one who thinks negatively and one who fails to conform to the Golden Rule and the Law of Love. He had developed the symptom for no other reason than that he felt he should be punished and should suffer for his sense of unworthiness and self-rejection, plus his hatred and antagonism for his foster father who had adopted him. I pointed out that his foster father had done the best he could for him and had played the dual role of a real father and mother. I told him he should forgive his foster father for his angry outburst.

He began to see the light immediately and perceived at the same time that he was punishing himself. When he drove me back to the hotel in Killarney, I gave him a copy of *The Power of Your Subconscious Mind* [1] and wrote out a special prayer for him to use several times daily, advising him also to continue cooperating with his physician.

Following is the prayer: "I release my foster father and my real father and mother, known only in Divine Mind, to God completely. I forgive myself for harboring negative and destructive thoughts about myself and others, and I resolve not to do this any more. Whenever negative thoughts come to me, I will immediately affirm, 'God's love fills my soul.' I am relaxed, poised, serene and calm. God guides my doctor in all his ministrations to me. The breath of the Almighty gave me life, and I know God breathed into me the breath of life and made me a living soul with all the powers and attributes of God within me. I inhale the peace of God and exhale the love of God, and God flows through me as harmony, joy, love, peace, wholeness and perfection."

I suggested that he affirm these great truths for about five minutes morning, afternoon and night, and that he be

[1]See *The Power of Your Subconscious Mind,* by Dr. Joseph Murphy, Prentice-Hall, Inc., Englewood Cliffs, New Jersey, 1963.

careful to never deny what he affirms. When fearful thoughts or approaching symptoms come, he is to say quietly, "I inhale the peace of God and I exhale the love of God to all."

On my return home to Beverly Hills, I received a lovely letter from him saying he has been completely free from all symptoms and has had no recurrence of any kind. Truly, the explanation is oftentimes the cure.

The Riches of Forgiveness

On a tour to the Shakespeare country, which takes you to Stratford-on-Avon in England, famous as the birthplace of William Shakespeare, and which has many associations with "The Immortal Bard," I chatted with a young lady during lunch in Warwick. During the course of the conversation, I said to her that I wrote along psychological and spiritual lines dealing with the problems of mankind. She was a nurse and had had a persistent skin rash for two years. She had consulted eminent dermatologists attached to the hospital where she worked, and they had prescribed various lotions and ointments, all to no avail.

We talked along psychosomatic lines, and I told her about the research work of Dr. Flanders Dunbar, author of *Emotions and Bodily Changes*[2] who says that the skin is where the inner and the outer worlds meet, and she chides her confreres when they fail to see that many skin conditions are caused by negative emotions such as hostility, resentment and other emotions inimical to our well-being. In other words, the skin is an organ of elimination, and mental poisons based on repressed emotions such as guilt, anxiety and remorse become translated into physical symptoms.

The young lady asked if she could come and have a conference with me before I left London, and I gladly consented to see her at the St. Ermin's Hotel, Caxton Street, where I always stay when visiting London.

---

[2]Published by Columbia University Press, New York, 1954. See also *Healing Beyond Medicine*, D. Snively, M.D., Parker Publishing Company, 1972.

The Cause of Her Itching and Persistent Skin Rash

I was quite frank with her and told her that I sensed she felt very guilty about something and believed in the need of punishment, and that if she confessed and cleansed her mind, the itching rash might well disappear. A bottled-up emotion repressed in the subconscious will sooner or later be translated into a bodily symptom. She confessed that she was married and that her husband was on a government assignment in India. During his absence she had been having sexual relations with her dentist, and she was full of remorse and guilt. She felt that God was punishing her for her sins.

Self-Forgiveness Brings Peace and Release

I explained to her that God, or the Life-Principle, never punishes, but that man punishes himself by his misuse of the laws of mind. For example, if you cut yourself, the Life Principle proceeds to form a blood clot called thrombin, and the subjective intelligence builds a bridge and forms new tissue. If you burn yourself, the Life-Principle holds no grudge, but it seeks to restore your skin to normal by reducing the edema, giving you new skin and tissue. If you take some bad food, the Life-Principle causes you to regurgitate it, as It always seeks to restore you to health. The tendency of the Life-Principle (God) is to heal, restore and make you whole.

Being a nurse, she understood all this. Then I asked a very pertinent question: "Do you want to be free of this rash?" Immediately she responded and said, "Yes." "Then," I said, "we have no problem. All you have to do is to stop doing what you are now doing and forgive yourself, and that's the end of your trouble." Accordingly, she came to a decision in my room in the hotel not to see the dentist any more and to cease condemning herself.

As I explained to her, self-condemnation and self-criticism are destructive mental poisons that send psychic pus all over the system, robbing one of vitality, vigor, wholeness and strength, leaving one a physical and mental wreck. I pointed out to her that all she had to do was to get all her thoughts to conform to the Divine Law of harmony and love. A new beginning is a new end.

We prayed together, claiming Divine love, peace and harmony were now saturating her entire being and that she was Divinely guided and watched over by an overshadowing Presence. In the silence, for about five minutes, we dwelt on one thing only — "The Healing Power of God's Love" — and then I reminded her of a great truth which should be indelibly imprinted in the minds and hearts of all: *This one thing I do, forgetting those things which are behind, and reaching forth unto those things which are before, I press toward the mark for the prize* (Philippians 3:13, 14).

The prize she sought was health, happiness and peace of mind. At the end of our meditation, the effulgence of an inner light glowed in her eyes and she felt something happen to her in the silence — the rash disappeared completely. We joined together in saying, *Father, I thank thee that thou hast heard me. And I know that thou hearest me always* (John 11:41, 42).

The Riches of Wisdom and Understanding

An old friend in London visited me at St. Ermin's Hotel and brought her boy of twelve, who is terribly afraid at night. Darkness seems to trouble him. This had been going on for two years. I asked the mother what had happened two years ago which had given a great shock to the boy which might be suppressed in his deeper mind, since the subconscious mind never forgets any experience, and that which we wanted to know about was the repressed emotion.

She recalled that two years previously the house they were living in in Liverpool had caught fire in the middle of the night, and the father had put his coat over the boy to protect him from the smoke. The boy exclaimed to me suddenly, "Daddy was suffocating me!" Actually, this was the answer to the whole problem.

We explained to the boy that his father was only trying to protect him and save his life, and that he should radiate love to his father and mother. I counselled the boy and his mother, explaining that no matter what had happened in the past, it could be changed now by filling the subconscious mind with life-giving patterns, as there is no time or space in mind, and that the lower is always subject to the higher. By filling the boy's mind with the truths of God, it would crowd out of his mind everything unlike God.

I gave the mother a prayer for her boy and asked the boy to use it also prior to sleep. This is the prayer the mother used:

"My boy is God's son. God loves him and cares for him. God's peace fills his soul. He is poised, serene, calm, relaxed and at ease. The joy of the Lord is his strength. The Healing Presence flows through him as harmony, peace, joy, love and perfection. God is, and His Presence vitalizes, energizes and restores his whole being to wholeness, beauty and perfection. He sleeps in peace and wakes in joy."

She changed the tense for the boy and had him repeat, "I am God's son," and so on. I told her to continue with the doctor and the prayers and to keep me informed. I was pleasantly surprised to receive a letter from the mother on my return to Beverly Hills saying, "My boy is healed. He had a vision in his sleep. A sage appeared and said to him, 'You are free. Tell your mother.' It was very vivid."

This was the subconscious of the boy revealing to him his healing. *I the Lord will make myself known unto him in a vision, and will speak unto him in a dream* (Numbers 12:6).

A MEDITATION FOR AN EFFECTIVE PROSPERITY PRAYER

Meditate often by repeating the following prayer for prosperity:

"'Thou shalt make thy way prosperous, and then thou shalt have good success.' I now give a pattern of success and prosperity to the deeper mind within me, which is the law. I now identify myself with the Infinite Source of supply. I listen to the still, small voice of God within me. This inner voice leads, guides and governs all my activities. I am one with the abundance of God. I know and believe that there are new and better ways of conducting my business; Infinite Intelligence reveals the new ways to me.

"I am growing in wisdom and understanding. My business is God's business. I am Divinely prospered in all ways. Divine Wisdom within me reveals the ways and means by which all my affairs are adjusted in the right way immediately.

"The words of faith and conviction which I now speak open up all the necessary doors or avenues for my success and prosperity. I know that 'The Lord (Law) will perfect that which concerneth me.' My feet are kept in the perfect path, because I am a son of the Living God."

CHAPTER POINTS TO REMEMBER

1. Resentment and hostility are mental poisons that rob you of vitality, enthusiasm and energy. Often refusal to eat means that the individual is slowly committing suicide, and this is a method of seeking revenge against someone else. The answer is to open the mind and heart to the influx of Divine love and to realize that others really do care and love you, bringing about a healing and a transformation.

2. When you begin to realize that you are an organ of God and that God hath need of you where you are, and that you are loved, needed and wanted, a complete transformation takes place; you begin to release the riches of the Infinite as love, goodwill, inner peace and abundance.

3. Often blind faith will bring about remarkable results. Paracelsus said, "Whether the object of your faith be true or false, you will get results." A young boy who stuttered fired his imagination into a joyous expectancy and blind faith and believed that if he slept in a bed where St. Kevin was supposed to have slept, he would be healed. His subconscious accepted his belief, and he was healed.

4. True faith consists of the belief that the Infinite Presence which created you knows all the processes and functions of your body, and that when you unite with It believingly, results will follow. True faith is the combined use of your conscious and subconscious mind, scientifically directed.

5. When you pray for health, then health should "spring forth speedily." If not, go to a doctor immediately and follow the injunction of the Bible, which says: *Honour a physician with the honour due unto him . . . for the Lord hath created him* (Ecclesiasticus, Chapter 38, Paragraph 1).

6. Some people experience excessive emotionalism at public healing meetings; it is a sort of mesmeric and emotional hysteria, and often there is a temporary alleviation of pain, and crippled people walk without crutches. Hypnotic suggestions have only temporary effect, however. In true healing, your conscious and subconscious mind must agree, and you must believe in your heart in the Infinite Healing Presence; then the result is permanent, not temporary. When you pray for healing, complete forgiveness must take place of all guilt, peeves and grudges. You know when you have forgiven others, because there is no sting in your mind.

7. There is no power in sticks, stones, amulets, charms, or bones of saints. But if a person believes that the bone of a dog is that of a saint and that if he kisses it a healing will follow, it is not the bone of the dog

that heals, it is a response of his subconscious mind to his blind belief.

8. Negative and destructive emotions snarl up in the subconscious mind and are the cause of many diseases. When a person feels guilty, he feels he should be punished, but what he fails to see is that he is punishing himself. When a boy's foster father died, he took on the symptoms of his foster father as a form of self-punishment for his guilt.

9. A wonderful prayer for forgiveness is this: "I forgive myself for harboring negative and destructive thoughts about myself and others, and I resolve not to do this any more. Whenever a negative thought comes to me, I will immediately affirm, 'God's love fills my soul.'"

10. Your skin is where the inner and the outer worlds meet, and emotions of hostility, anger, suppressed rage and resentment may be translated into many skin diseases. Remorse and guilt, according to psychosomatic physicians, are the cause of many skin eruptions.

11. The Life Principle (God) never punishes. This Presence always seeks to heal you and to make you whole. Self-condemnation and self-criticism are destructive mental poisons that send psychic pus all over your system, leaving you a physical and mental wreck.

12. Come to a decision. Forget the past and saturate your mind with Divine love, peace and harmony. Realize Divine love dissolves everything unlike itself.

13. No matter what has happened in the past, you can change it now. Fill your subconscious with life-giving patterns of thought and you will erase and crowd out everything unlike God.

14. The meditation at the end of the chapter will help you to improve your life and make your way prosperous.

five

How Dialing Miracle Thought-Forms Will Increase Your Wealth

The whole world and all its treasures in the sea, air and earth were here when you were born. Begin to think of the untold and undiscovered riches all around you, waiting for the intelligence of man to bring them forth. A sales manager said to me the other day that an associate of his sold a million dollar idea for expansion to the organization; he also added that there were more millionaires now in the United States than at any time in history. You can have an idea worth a fortune! Moreover, you are here to release the imprisoned splendor within you and *surround yourself with luxury, beauty and the riches of life.*

Make Friends with Money and You Will Always Have Money

In this book, you will learn that it is necessary to have the right attitude toward money. When you really make friends with money, you will always have a surplus of it. It is normal and natural for you to desire a fuller, richer, happier and more wonderful life. Look upon money as God's idea of maintaining the economic health of the nations of the world. When money is circulating freely in your life, you are economically healthy, in the same manner as when your blood is circulating freely, you are free from congestion. Begin now to see money in its true significance and role in life as a symbol of exchange. Money to you should mean freedom from want; it should mean beauty, luxury, abundance, sense of security and refinement.

Why She Did Not Have More Money

Being poor is a mental attitude. A young lady, a very good writer who had had several articles accepted for publication, said to me, "I don't write for money." I said to her, "What's wrong with money? It's true you don't write for money, but the laborer is worthy of his hire. What you write inspires, lifts up, and encourages others. When you adopt the right attitude, financial compensation will automatically come to you freely and copiously."

She actually disliked money. Once she referred to money as "filthy lucre." *She had a subconscious pattern that there was some virtue in poverty.* I explained to her that there was no evil in the universe and that good and evil were in the thoughts and motivations of man. All evil comes from misinterpretation of life and misuse of the laws of mind. In other words, the only evil is ignorance, and the only consequence is suffering.

It would be foolish to pronounce uranium, silver, lead, copper, iron, cobalt, nickel, calcium or a dollar bill evil. The only difference between one metal and another is the number and rate of motion of electrons revolving around a central nucleus. A piece of paper such as a $100 bill is innocuous, and the only difference between it and copper or lead is that the atoms and molecules with their electrons and protons are arranged differently for the physical evidences of money.

She Adopted New Ideas Toward
Money and Prospered Accordingly

Here is a simple technique she practiced, which multiplied money in her experience: "My writings go forth to bless, heal, inspire, elevate and dignify the minds and hearts of men and women, and I am Divinely compensated in a wonderful way. I look upon money as Divine substance, for everything is made from the One Spirit. I know matter and spirit are one. Money is constantly circulating in my life, and I use it wisely and constructively. Money flows to me freely, joyously and endlessly. Money is an idea in the mind of God, and it is good and very good."

This young lady's changed attitude toward money has worked wonders in her life, and she has completely eradicated that strange, superstitious belief that money was "filthy lucre." She realized that her silent condemnation of money caused money to fly from her instead of to her. Her income has tripled in three months, which was just the beginning of her financial prosperity.

He Worked Hard But Lacked Money

Some years ago, I talked with a minister who had a very good following. He had an excellent knowledge of the laws of mind and was able to impart this knowledge to others, but *he* could never make ends meet! He had what he thought was a good alibi for his plight by quoting from Timothy: *For the love of money is the root of all evil* (I Timothy 6:10), forgetting what followed in the 17th verse of the same chapter, when Paul charges the people to place their trust or faith in the living God, *who giveth us richly all things to enjoy* (I Timothy 6:17).

Love in Biblical language is to give your allegiance, loyalty and faith to the Source of all things, which is God. You are not, therefore, to give your allegiance, loyalty and trust to created things, but to the Creator, the Eternal Source of everything in the universe. If a man says, "All I want is money, nothing else. That's my god and nothing but money matters," he can get it, of course, but he is here to lead a balanced life. Man must also claim peace, harmony, beauty, guidance, love, joy and wholeness in all phases of his life.

To make money the sole aim in life would constitute an error or wrong choice. You must express your hidden talents, find your true place in life and experience the joy of contributing to the growth, happiness and success of others. As you study this book and apply the laws of your subconscious in the right way, you can have all the money you want and still have peace of mind, harmony, wholeness and serenity. To accumulate money to the exclusion of everything else causes man to become lopsided and unbalanced.

I pointed out to this minister how he was completely misinterpreting the Scripture in pronouncing pieces of paper or metals evil, when these were neutral substances, for there is nothing good or bad but thinking makes it so. He began to see all the good he could do with more money for his wife, family and parishioners. He changed his attitude and let go of his superstition. He began to claim boldly, regularly and systematically, "Infinite Spirit reveals better ways for me to serve. I am inspired and illumined, and I give a Divine transfusion of faith and confidence in the One Presence and Power to all those who hear me. I look upon money as God's idea, and it is constantly circulating in my life and that of my parishioners. We use it wisely, judiciously and constructively under God's guidance and wisdom."

This young minister made a habit of this prayer, knowing that it would activate the powers of his subconscious mind. Today he has a beautiful church which the people built for him. He has a radio program and has all the money he needs for his personal worldly and cultural needs. I can assure you, he no longer criticizes money.

The Master Key and Program to Disciplining Your Mind for Money

If you follow the procedure and technique outlined herein, you will never want for money all the days of your life.

Step 1: Reason it out in your mind that God, or the Life-Principle, is the Source of the universe, the galaxies in space, and everything you see, whether you look at the stars in the sky, the mountains, the lakes, the deposits in the earth and sea, or all animals and plants. The Life-Principle gave birth to you, and all the powers, qualities and attributes of God are within you. Come to a simple conclusion that everything you see and are aware of came out of the invisible mind of God, or Life, and that everything that man has invented, created or made came out of the invisible mind of man; and the mind of man and the mind of God are one, for there is only one mind common to all individual men. Come now to a clear-cut decision that God is the Source of your supply of energy, vitality, health, creative ideas, the Source of the sun, the air you breathe, the apple you eat, and the money in your pocket, for everything is made inside and out of the Invisible. It is as easy for God to become wealth in your life as it is to become a blade of grass.

Step 2: Decide now to engrave in your subconscious mind the idea of wealth. Ideas are conveyed to the subconscious by repetition, faith and expectancy. By repeating a thought pattern or an act over and over again, it becomes automatic, and, your subconscious being compulsive, you will be compelled to express it. The pattern is the same as learning to walk, swim, play the piano, type, etc. You must *believe* in what you are affirming. Realize that what you are affirming is like the apple seeds you deposit in the ground, and they grow after their kind. By watering and fertilizing these seeds, you accelerate their growth. Know what you are doing and why you are doing it.

Step 3: Repeat the following affirmation for about five minutes night and morning: "I am now writing in my subconscious mind the idea of God's wealth. God is the Source of my supply, and all my needs are met at every moment of time and point of space. God's wealth flows freely, joyously and ceaselessly into my experience, and I give thanks for God's riches forever circulating in my experience."

Step 4: When thoughts of lack come to you, such as, "I can't afford that trip," or, "I can't meet that note at the bank," or, "I can't pay that bill," *never finish a negative statement* about finances. Reverse it immediately in your mind by affirming, "God is my instant and everlasting supply, and that bill is paid in Divine order." If a negative thought comes to you fifty times in one hour, reverse it each time by thinking, "God is my instant supply, meeting that need right now." After a while, the thought of financial lack will lose all momentum and you will find your subconscious is being conditioned to wealth. If you look at a new car, for example, *never say,* "I can't buy that." On the contrary, say to yourself: "That car is for sale. It is a Divine idea, and I accept it in Divine Order."

This is the master key. When applied as outlined in the above program, the law of opulence will work for you as well as for anybody else. The law of mind is no respecter of persons. Your thoughts make you wealthy or poor. Choose the riches of life right here and right now.

A Salesman Moves Up from $5,000 to $25,000 in One Year

A sales manager sent me one of his men for counseling. This salesman was a brilliant college graduate and knew his products very well. He was in a lucrative territory but was making only about $5,000 annually in commissions. The sales manager felt he should double or triple that.

In talking to the young man, I found he was down on himself. He had developed a subconscious pattern of $5,000 a year. He said that he had been born in a poverty-stricken home and that his parents had told him that he was destined to be poor. His step-father had always told him, "You'll never amount to anything." *These thoughts were accepted by his impressionable mind,* and he was experiencing his subconscious belief in lack and limitation.

I explained to him that he could change his subconscious by feeding it with life-giving patterns. Accordingly, I gave him a mental and spiritual formula to follow which would transform his life. I explained to him that he should under no circumstances deny what he affirmed, because his subconscious mind accepted what he really believed.

He affirmed every morning before going to work: "I'm born to succeed; the Infinite within me can't fail. Divine law and order govern my life, Divine peace fills my soul, Divine love saturates my mind. Infinite Intelligence guides me in all ways. God's riches flow to me freely. I am advancing, moving forward and growing mentally, spiritually, financially and in all other ways. I know these truths are sinking into my subconscious mind and will grow after their kind."

The Results

A year later when I met this young man again, I discovered that he had been transformed. He had absorbed these ideas which we had discussed, and he said, "I am appreciating life now, and wonderful things have happened. I have had an income of $25,000 this year, five times greater than the previous year." He has learned the simple truth that whatever he inscribes in his subconscious mind becomes effective and functional in his life.

MEDITATION FOR A RICH HARVEST OF FINANCIAL WEALTH

Use the following meditation for assurance in achieving financial wealth:

"'Thou madest him to have dominion over the works of thy hands.' I know that my faith in God determines my future. My faith in God means my faith in all things good. I unite myself now with true ideas and I know the future will be in the image and likeness of my habitual thinking. 'As a man thinketh in his heart so is he.' From this moment forward my thoughts are on: 'Whatsoever things are true, whatsoever things are honest, whatsoever things are just, whatsoever things are lovely, and of good report'; day and night I meditate on these things and I know these seeds (thoughts) which I habitually dwell upon will become a rich harvest for me. I am the captain of my own soul; I am the master of my fate; for my thought and feeling are my destiny."

CHAPTER POINTS TO REMEMBER

1. Begin to think of the untold riches all around you, waiting for the intelligence of man to reveal them. There is a guiding principle within you which, when called upon, will reveal to you the riches you are seeking.

2. There is an old saying: "Make friends with money and you will always have it." Look upon money as God's idea, circulating among nations, maintaining economic health. Claim that money is circulating in your life, and your subconscious will see to it that you have all the money you need.

3. If you condemn money, calling it "filthy lucre," the root of all evil, and making other such nonsensical statements, your money will take wings and fly away. Money, like everything else in the universe, is universal substance, which is Spirit reduced to the point of visibility. Money, like nickel, cobalt, iron, platinum, lead, oil and coal, are all forms of the universal substance operating at different frequencies and vibrations.

4. Adopt a new attitude toward money, realizing you are entitled to be richly compensated for your work, whether it be writing, teaching, gardening,

or whatever. Think of all the good you can do when money is circulating freely in your life.

5. You can work very hard, but if you dislike money or criticize it, you will find yourself in want financially. You do not make a god of money, but you realize that it is essential on this three-dimensional plane. You look to the real *Source* of wealth, which is God, and you know that as you turn to the Source It will turn to you and give you all the riches of life. In other words, you don't worship a created thing. You worship the Creator; your expectation is from God, who giveth to all life, breath and all things richly to enjoy.

6. Claim that you are always using money wisely, judiciously and constructively for your own good and that of all men and women everywhere. Constantly claim also that the Infinite reveals better ways in which you can serve.

7. The master key to disciplining the mind for money is to come to a clear-cut decision once and for all that God is the source of everything you see in the universe, and that everything man has made came also out of the mind of God. Believing this to be true, your affirmation for wealth will prove productive. When fearful thoughts or thoughts of lack come to your mind, reverse them at once by affirming, "God is my instant supply — that bill is paid in Divine mind now," or any similar appropriate affirmation. The *secret* is *never* finish a negative statement regarding finances. After a while, the negative thoughts will cease to come, and you find you have conditioned your subconscious to wealth.

8. A salesman advanced from $5,000 to $25,000 in a year by changing his attitude of mind toward himself and money. His subconscious belief in poverty had held him back. He began to feed his sub-

conscious mind with thoughts of success, opulence, right action and abundance; and he discovered that his thought, when properly guided, created promotion, wealth, self-esteem and recognition from his superiors and customers. He learned that what he inscribes in his subconscious becomes effective and functional in his life. His journey is now ever onward, upward and Godward.

9. Use the meditation at the end of the chapter to assure yourself of a rich financial harvest.

six

How to Say the Exact Words That Will Bring You Money

Bring joy into your life. Pray for joy by claiming it. Affirm: "The joy of the Lord is my strength." But don't keep analyzing it or gritting your teeth about it. Just know that "joy" is the *elan* of life, the expression of life. Don't work "like a horse" at it. No will power, no muscle power, no blood vessel power is involved in this mental and spiritual therapeutic technique. *Just know and claim* that the joy of the Lord is flowing through you now and wonders will happen as you pray this way. Freedom and peace of mind will be yours as a result.

How She Enriched Herself Through Effective Prayer

A woman said to me: "I was blocked financially. I had reached the point where I had not enough money for food for the children. All I had was $5. I held it in my hand and said, 'God will multiply this exceedingly according to his riches in glory, and I am now filled with the riches of God.

All my needs are instantaneously met now and all the days of my life.' I affirmed this for about half an hour, and a great sense of peace came over me. I spent the $5 freely for food. The owner of the market asked me if I wanted to work there as a cashier, since the present one had just gotten married and left. I accepted it, and shortly afterwards I married the owner (my boss), and we have experienced and are experiencing all the riches of life."

This woman looked to the Source; she believed in her heart, and the blessings of the Infinite followed. Her good was magnified and multiplied exceedingly.

How Her Prayer for Her Students Worked Wonders

Chatting with a teacher while traveling to Hawaii, she told me that she was a teacher of Spanish and French in a religious institution and that every morning all of them would join together, each one of the students affirming aloud: "I am inspired from On High. Infinite Intelligence leads and guides me in my studies. I pass all my examinations in Divine order. I radiate love and goodwill to all my classmates. I am happy, joyous and free. God loves me and cares for me."

She said that a tremendous change has taken place in her students and that not a single one has failed in her classes for the past three years. She stated that she gives them a transfusion of faith and confidence in the Almighty every morning by telling them that they will pass, that they will be guided in their studies, and that they will have a perfect memory for everything they need to know. The students listen to her, absorb the truth of her statement, and together with their morning affirmations, these truths sink into their subconscious mind; and according to the impression in their subconscious, is it done unto them.

She is a wise teacher who has discovered that scientific prayer works wonders and miracles in an endless number of ways.

How Effective Prayer Enabled
Him to Make a Comeback

A sales manager told me that he had been fired because of excessive drinking on the job and because of being involved with one of the secretaries in the office. He was very distressed, dejected, and worried about his wife, his income and his future.

In talking with his wife later, I discovered that she was a chronic nagger and had tried unsuccessfully to dominate and control her husband. She was abnormally jealous and very possessive, and she clocked him in every evening, creating a scene if he were not home at a certain hour.

He was emotionally and spiritually immature and did not handle the matter at all constructively. He deeply resented her nagging and her clocking of his arrival at home and retaliated by drinking and becoming involved with another woman. He said to me, "I just wanted to get even with her."

Both of them agreed to start a prayer process night and morning, realizing that as they prayed for each other there could not possibly be any bitterness, hostility or resentment, as Divine love casts out everything unlike itself.

She prayed night and morning as follows: "My husband is God's man. God is guiding him to his true place. What he is seeking is seeking him. God's love fills his soul and God's peace fills his mind and heart. God prospers him in all ways. There are harmony, peace, love and understanding between us. It is God in action in our lives."

He likewise prayed for his wife night and morning as follows: "My wife is God's child. God loves her and cares for her. God's love, peace, harmony and joy flow through her at all times and she is Divinely guided in all ways. There are harmony, peace, love and understanding between us. I see God in her and she sees God in me."

How It All Worked Out

As both of them became relaxed and peaceful about the situation, they realized that "only good can come out of the situation." Soon he received a phone call from the president of the company, calling him back, stating that he had heard he had had a reconciliation with his wife, and at the same time he praised him for his past achievements and accomplishments for the organization.

Actually, his wife, without his knowledge, had visited the president and had told him the whole story, how happy they now were, and how the "other woman" had vanished out of his life. She told how they were now praying together. He was deeply impressed, and she and her husband discovered very quickly the riches of scientific prayer.

Let the Riches of the Infinite Flow Through You

Constantly affirm, feel and believe that God multiplies your good exceedingly and you will be enriched every moment of the day spiritually, mentally, intellectually, financially and socially, for there is no end to the glory of man for his daily living. Watch the wonders that will happen as you impress these truths in your subconscious mind. You will experience a glorious future, even in a financial way.

The Sure Riches of "Watch and Pray"

Watch your thoughts. Never talk about economic lack and limitation; never talk about your being poor or in want. It is very foolish to talk to your neighbors or relatives about hard times, financial problems and like matters. Count your blessings. Begin to think prosperous thoughts; talk about God's riches present everywhere. Realize that the feeling of wealth produces wealth. When you talk about not having enough to go around, and how little you have, and how you must cut corners and eat the cheapest meat, these thoughts are creative and *you are only impoverishing yourself.*

Use the money you now have freely; release it with joy and realize that God's wealth flows to you in avalanches of abundance. Look up to the Source. As you turn to God, the response will come, as "He careth for you." You will find neighbors, strangers and associates adding to your good and also to your supply of material things. Make it a practice to pray for Divine guidance in all your ways and believe that God is supplying all your needs according to His riches in glory. As you make a habit of this attitude of mind, you will find the invisible law of opulence can and will produce visible riches for you.

She Became a Tremendous Success Through Effective Prayer

A beauty parlor operator told me that the secret of her success was that every morning prior to opening her beauty salon, she had a quiet period in which she affirms: "God's peace fills my soul and God's love saturates my whole being. God guides, prospers and inspires me. I am illumined and His healing love flows from me to all my clients. Divine love comes in my door and Divine love goes out of my door. All those who come into my salon are blessed, healed and inspired. The Infinite Healing Presence saturates the whole place. This is the day the Lord hath made, and I rejoice and give thanks for the countless blessings which come to my clients and to myself."

She had this prayer written out on a card and reiterates these truths every morning. At night she gives thanks for all her clients, claiming that they are guided, prospered, happy and harmonious and that God and His love flow through each one, filling up all the empty vessels in her life.

She stated to me that following this prayer technique pattern, at the end of three months she had far more clients than she could handle and had to hire three additional operators! She had discovered the riches of effective prayer and is prospering beyond her fondest dreams.

Realize the Rich Blessings of the Infinite

Recently a doctor in Beverly Hills said to me that her constant prayer was as follows: "I live in the joyous expectancy of the best, and invariably the best comes to me. My favorite Bible verse with which I saturate my mind is: *He giveth to all life, and breath, and all things* (Acts 17:25)." She has learned that *she is not dependent on people* for joy, health, success and happiness or peace of mind. She looks to the Living Spirit Almighty within her for promotion, achievement, wealth, success and happiness. *Whosoever trusteth in the Lord, happy is he* (Proverbs 16:20).

Contemplate promotion, success, achievement, illumination and inspiration, and the Spirit of the Almighty will move on your behalf, compelling you to express fully what you meditate on. Let go now, and permit the Infinite riches of the Infinite One to open up new doors for you, and let wonders happen in your life.

The Riches of Effective Prayer Therapy

In prayer therapy, avoid struggle and strain, since this attitude is indicative of your unbelief. In your subconscious is all the wisdom and power necessary to solve any problem. Your conscious mind is prone to look at external conditions and tends continually to struggle and to resist. Remember, however, *it is the quiet mind that gets things done.* Quiet your body periodically; tell it to be still and relax, and it will obey you. When your conscious mind is quiet and receptive, the wisdom of your subconscious mind rises to the surface mind and you receive your solution.

How Do You Feel After Prayer?

You can know if you have succeeded in prayer by the way you feel. If you remain worried or anxious, and if you are wondering how, when, where or through what source your answer will come, you are meddling. This indicates you do not really trust the wisdom of your subconscious. Avoid nagging yourself all day long or even from time to time. When you think of your desire, lightness of touch is important; remind yourself that Infinite Intelligence is taking care of it in Divine order far better than you can by tenseness of your conscious mind.

How Often Should You Pray?

Many people ask: "How often should I pray for a loved one who is ill, who is in the hospital, or who is impoverished financially?" The general answer is that you should pray until you feel satisfied within, or you just feel that this is the best you can do for the time being. Expect your prayer for harmony, wholeness, vitality and abundance to be answered. You may pray later on during the day, as soon as you have gotten away from the last prayer. You will know when your prayer is answered by experiencing an inner sense of peace and certitude, followed by no further desire to pray.

Long sessions of prayer are usually a mistake, as they may indicate you are trying to force things by using mental coercion, which always results in the opposite of what you are praying for. You will often find that a short prayer uttered from the heart gets better results than a long prayer.

He Restoreth My Soul (Psalm 23:3)

Learn to let go and relax. Do not give power to the ailment or condition. Give power and allegiance to the Infinite Healing Presence. The swimming instructor tells you that you can float on the water, which will support you if you remain quiet, still and at peace. But if you get nervous or fearful, you will sink.

When you are seeking a spiritual healing, feel that you are immersed in the Holy Omnipresence, and that the Golden River of life, love, truth and beauty is flowing through you, transforming your whole being into the pattern of harmony, health and peace. Identify yourself with the river of life and love, and feel yourself swimming in the great ocean of life. That sense of oneness with God will restore you. *He restoreth my soul* (Psalm 23:3).

MEDITATION FOR A WONDERFUL FUTURE

The following meditation used daily will bring you many wonderful things:

"I know that I mold, fashion and create my own destiny. My faith in God is my destiny; this means an abiding faith in all things good. I live in the joyous expectancy of the best; only the best comes to me. I know the harvest I will reap in the future, because all my thoughts are God's thoughts, and God is with my thoughts of good. My thoughts are the seeds of goodness, truth and beauty. I now place my thoughts of love, peace, joy, success and goodwill in the garden of my mind. This is God's garden and it will yield an abundant harvest. The glory and beauty of God will be expressed in my life. From this moment forward, I express life, love and truth. I am radiantly happy and prosperous in all ways. Thank you, Father."

CHAPTER POINTS TO REMEMBER

1. Whatever money you have, bless it now and believe it when you say, "God will multiply this exceedingly now and forevermore." Believe it in your heart and you will never want all the days of your life.

2. When a husband and wife pray for each other, exalting God in the midst of one another and claiming peace, harmony, love and inspiration for one another, all resentment and ill will are dissolved, and both will prosper. If you are fired from a position, claim, "Only good can come out of this" and you will discover a new door opens up a far more wonderful position than the previous one.

3. Focus your attention on whatsoever things are lovely, noble, wonderful and God-like, and you will experience the riches of life. Remember, you reap what you sow in your subconscious.

4. Watch your thoughts. Your thoughts are creative. Never talk about lack, limitation, or being poor, or unable to make ends meet. This multiplies your misery. Think of God's riches and affirm boldly that the riches of the Infinite are flowing to you in avalanches of abundance. Claim it boldly and the Infinite will respond.

5. A beauty parlor operator became an outstanding success by affirming regularly and systematically: "God's peace fills my soul and God's love saturates my whole being. His healing love flows from me to all my clients. All those who come into my salon are blessed, healed, prospered and inspired." She made a habit of this prayer and has prospered beyond her fondest dreams.

6. A wonderful prayer enabling you to experience the riches of the Infinite is this: "I live in the joyous expectancy of the best and invariably the best comes to me. *God giveth to all life, and breath, and all things (Acts 17:25)."*

7. In teaching students, realize that Infinite Intelligence is guiding and directing them in their studies. Claim that they pass all their examinations in Divine order. Give them a transfusion of faith and confidence in the Power within them, and you will be amazed how they pick up your conviction of them subconsciously. Wonders happen as you pray this way.

8. Assure yourself of a full, rich future by using the meditation at the end of the chapter.

seven

How to Activate the
Psychic Money-Machine

"To prosper" means to succeed, to thrive, to turn out well. In other words, when you are prospering, you are expanding, growing spiritually, mentally, financially, socially and intellectually. In order to truly prosper, it is necessary that you become a channel through which the Life-Principle flows freely, harmoniously, joyously and lovingly. I suggest that you establish a definite method of working and thinking and that you practice it regularly and systematically every day.

How Prosperity Thoughts Changed His Life

One young man who consulted with me had experienced a "poverty complex" for many years and had received no answers to his prayers. He had prayed for prosperity, but the fear of poverty continuously weighed on his mind and, naturally, he attracted more lack and limitation than prosperity. The subconscious mind accepts the dominant of two ideas.

After talking with me, he began to realize that his thought-image of wealth produces wealth, and that every thought is creative *unless it is neutralized by a counter thought of greater intensity.* Furthermore, he realized that his thought and belief about poverty was greater than his belief in the infinite riches all around him. Consequently, he changed his thoughts and kept them changed. I wrote out a prosperity prayer for him, as follows (I know it will benefit you also):

An Effective Prosperity Prayer

"I know there is only one Source, the Life-Principle, from which all things flow. It created the universe and all things therein contained. I am a focal point of the Divine Presence. My mind is open and receptive. I am a free-flowing channel for harmony, beauty, guidance, wealth and the riches of the Infinite. I know that health, wealth and success are released from within and appear on the without. I am now in harmony with the infinite riches within and without, and I know these thoughts are sinking into my subconscious mind and will be reflected on the screen of space. I wish for everyone all the blessings of life. I am open and receptive to God's riches — spiritual, mental and material — and they flow to me in avalanches of abundance."

His Changed Thinking Suddenly Changed Him into a Prosperous Person

This young man focused his thoughts on God's riches rather than on poverty and made it a special point not to deny what he affirmed. In a month's time, his whole life was transformed. He affirmed the above truths morning and evening for about ten minutes, knowing that he was actually writing down these truths in his subconscious mind, causing the latter to be activated and to release its hidden treasures. Although he had been a salesman for ten years with rather dim prospects for the future, suddenly he was made sales manager at $30,000 a year plus prime benefits.

How She Wrote Her Desires in Her Prayerful
Heart and Received Astounding Results

A young woman learned that her conscious mind could be likened to a pen and that she could inscribe her true desires on her subconscious by frequent habitation of the mind with the desires of her heart. Accordingly, she decided to write two desires in her deeper mind by thinking of each one separately and with interest, knowing that her subconscious would respond exactly according to the impression made upon it.

Her Most Cherished Desires

Her first desire was as follows: "My mother and I are going on a two-week holiday to Mexico. We have agreed that Infinite Intelligence opens up the way in Divine order." Both of them pictured themselves on the plane, and they conducted an animated conversation in their imaginations with the hostesses. They felt the tangibility of the plane and the naturalness of the whole thing.

After about a week, this young woman came to my office all excited, saying, "Look what I found — this envelope on the street containing twenty 100 dollar bills and a note inside: 'Whoever finds this, keep it. God bless you,' and that's all." There was no name or any identification of any kind on the envelope. Now, it happens that there are eccentric millionaires who do things like this from time to time, which is a possible explanation of her good fortune. They went on a wonderful extended tour of Mexico. The ways of your subconscious to get results are truly past finding out.

Her *second desire* was for *marriage*. This is what she wrote with her conscious mind pen in her subconscious: "I know my desire for marriage and happiness is the voice of God in me urging me to lead a full and happy life. I know that I am one with the Infinite now. I know and believe there is a man waiting to love and cherish me. I know I can contribute to his happiness and peace. I can be a great asset to him. I can cherish, love and inspire him to greatness. He loves my ideals and I love his ideals. He does not want to make me over; neither do I want to make him over. There are mutual love, freedom and respect between us. These words go forth and accomplish whereunto they are sent. I have written this request in my subconscious mind with faith and confidence, and I decree it is done, finished and established in my deeper mind. Whenever I think of marriage, I shall remind myself that infinite intelligence of my subconscious is bringing this to pass in Divine order."

A few weeks went by and the dentist who had been working on her teeth for some weeks suddenly proposed to her and she accepted. I had the joy and satisfaction of performing the marriage ceremony. This young woman gained a new insight into the wonders of her subconscious mind. *Think prosperous* and wholesome thoughts, *and wonders happen* as you pray.

How Riches of Daily Healthy Thinking Brought Great Benefits

A young, divorced woman was resisting life by complaining, "I am leading a humdrum existence. I am lonesome, frustrated, and I have no friends. I lead a drab, weary existence," etc. However, she learned that her thoughts are creative and that by thinking negatively along the above lines, she was actually compounding her misery, because whatever we give attention to, the subconscious magnifies and multiplies in our experience.

After learning something about the laws of mind in our interviews, she reversed her habitual frustrated thinking and began to affirm frequently and systematically: "I am happy, joyous and free. I am loving, kind, harmonious and peaceful. I sing the song of praise in the Lord, which is my strength."

She realized and understood the mental law that whatever she attached to "I AM," she would manifest and express. She made a habit of affirming the above mental truths, and her whole life was changed from the former so-called drab existence to a fullness of life, including marriage to a brilliant engineer, a new home, plus a new perspective and a new insight into the wonders of the riches within her.

How a Housewife Planned for Prosperity and Happiness and Got Results

A housewife who conferred with me was constantly whining and complaining, "There is no happiness for me. I was born on the wrong side of the tracks. I am stuck to a treadmill sort of existence. I wash, cook, iron, scrub, wash dishes and windows, and take care of three children." She was resenting and resisting her environment and felt life was against her and unkind to her.

During our discussion, however, she began to awaken to the truth that prosperity and happiness represent a state of mind. Accordingly, she reversed her way of thinking and began to claim, "Divine right action is mine. Success is mine. Wealth is mine. Happiness is mine. God's river of peace governs my mind, body, and activities, and whatever I do will prosper. I know my thoughts are creative. As an engineer plans a bridge, so am I planning prosperity and happiness now. I believe implicitly in the law of the Bible, which promises, *Ask, and it shall be given you; seek, and ye shall find; knock, and it shall be opened unto you* (Matthew 7:7)."

This housewife accordingly stirred up the gift of God's prosperity within her, and her relationship to her work, her home and her children changed. She released the imprisoned splendors within. Money came in from totally unexpected sources and she became completely satisfied with her new lot in life.

There Are Beauty and Abundance Where You Are

God is indescribable beauty, and God indwells you; He walks and talks in you. Your mind and your spirit, your thoughts and your feelings all represent God within you. The invisible life and power within you is God. Your thought, being creative, is also God in action in your life. Begin to contemplate that God's beauty and riches flow through your thoughts, words and deeds, and you will pass on the beauty and riches of God to your family, friends and neighbors. Give thanks for all the blessings you have. You can make your home beautiful and you can inspire others to experience the riches of your deeper mind. You are the artist, the weaver, the designer and the architect of your life.

The Riches of His Secret Plan for Making a Profitable Business Deal

I know of a man operating a large market whose brother, a partner, had recently died. This brother had bequeathed his one-half interest in the business to his two nieces. These girls were very negative and demanding, creating all sorts of problems for this man. They refused to sell their one-half interest. He said to me that following an argument with them over more money from the business, he wrote down on a piece of paper, "I loose these girls to God completely. They are in their true place. Nothing is forever. This condition passes away *now*. It is God in action." He placed this writing in a drawer in his desk, which was marked "With God all things are possible," and forgot about it. In two weeks' time, the two girls (his nieces) agreed to sell their interest and there was a perfect harmonious solution for his getting a profitable deal for the whole business.

His technique was sound. Actually, he was writing the solution in his subconscious mind, and his method of placing it in a drawer in his desk was simply an *outer symbol.* He released his problem to the infinite intelligence of his subconscious mind, which is the secret place from which you draw forth the answer to all your problems.

How to Consider the Riches of the Infinite

You can look at the stars at night, the cumulus clouds are there for you to admire, and the sky is as blue for you as it is for everyone. You can look at the sunset whether you are rich or poor. You can listen to the songs of the birds and become enraptured with the beauty all around you. Begin to see the Divine Presence in all things about you — in the rising sun, the golden moon, the sky, the mountains, the rivers, the rivulets and the streams. Contemplate the beauty of all nature, and don't forget to see the love in your dog's eyes.

Life is a mirror which reflects back to us precisely that which we deposit in our minds. Look through the eyes of love and beauty, and love, beauty and the riches of the Infinite will come back to you. Longfellow said, "Look not mournfully into the past; it comes not back again. Wisely improve the present; it is the thing. Go forth to meet the shadowy future without fear and a manly heart." Seneca said, "We can only say he is anxious about the future to whom the present is unprofitable." God (your good) is the Eternal Now! Claim your good and all the riches of life now. What you can conceive, you can achieve through the wisdom and power of your subconscious mind.

The Wonders of Prosperous and Healthy Writing Out of Your Desires

Every New Year's Eve, I am requested to preside at an assembly and to conduct a New Year's prayer for a group of men and their wives. The custom is that each person writes out clearly his or her desires of the heart. There are only four categories, such as health, wealth, love and expression. No matter what you seek comes under one of these classifications. If, for example, you request wisdom as your sole desire, that comes under expression, or your desire to release more and more of the life, love, truth, beauty and riches of the deeper mind. Also in writing down their desires, it was suggested that a friend or relative be included in one of them. For example, if the friend or relative was involved in a lawsuit, they were instructed to write down: "There is a Divine and harmonious solution through the infinite justice and harmony of God for ———."

How Desires Written Out Have
Come to Be Fulfilled

It is amazing how many of these desires are answered before the end of the year. In many instances some of their prayers are answered early the following year, but then it happens that the answers actually come at the right time, i.e., when they are ready. All these written requests are placed in sealed envelopes and given to one of the men present, who places them in his safe at home; and on the following New Year's Eve, each one is presented with his or her envelope and the owner reads it privately.

One man showed me his written request and said every one had been fulfilled in Divine order. One of his desires was that he would have more time for his sons and for more recreation and travel with his family. He was transferred and promoted and received six weeks' vacation, enabling him to take his family on a five-week cruise. Also, he had much more time for his family during the week.

Another request by a mother was that her two sons would never be called to service. They were deeply spiritual boys and abhorred war. They have never been called and, as she said, they never will be. She decreed and wrote, "My boys are God's sons. God places them in their true place where they are doing what they love to do. God knows and God cares."

All these men and women write down the deepest desires of their hearts, trusting and believing that the infinite intelligence in their subconscious mind will bring their desires to pass in Divine order. I always conclude my prayer with the group in this way: "We decree that all these written desires are inscribed in the subconscious of each and that all these desires come forth in Divine law and order."

These prayers are answered either as written or in a grander and greater way in the sight of the Higher-Self, which knows all and sees all. All these men and women are amazed to see the wonderful way in which these prayers are answered.

The Real Secret of It All

The secret purpose of writing these desires and sealing them is that we release them completely to the wisdom of the subconscious with faith and confidence, knowing that as the sun rises in the morning, so will there be a resurrection of all these desires in Divine order. This is called Divine indifference. When you have this attitude of mind, your prayers are always answered. Divine indifference means that you know it is impossible for your prayer to fail, for it is written, *He will not fail thee, nor forsake thee* (Deuteronomy 31:6).

MEDITATION FOR IMPREGNATING YOUR SUBCONSCIOUS MIND

The following meditation sincerely believed by you and repeated often will yield you great treasures:

"'Be ye doers of the word, and not hearers only, deceiving yourselves.' My creative word is my silent conviction that my prayer is answered. When I speak the word for healing, success or prosperity, my word is spoken in the consciousness of Life and Power, knowing that it is done. My word has power, because it is one with Omnipotence. The words I speak are always constructive and creative. When I pray, my words are full of life, love and feeling; this makes my affirmations, thoughts and words creative. I know the greater my faith behind the word spoken, the more power it has. The words I use form a definite mold which determine what form my thought is to take. Divine Intelligence operates through me now and reveals to me what I need to know. I have the answer now. I am at peace. God is Peace."

CHAPTER POINTS TO REMEMBER

1. You are prospering when you are expanding along all lines spiritually, mentally, intellectually and

financially. You should have all the money you need to do what you want to do and when you want to do it.

2. **Your subconscious mind accepts the dominant of two ideas.** Reason out clearly all the reasons why all things visible and invisible come from One Source. All things made by man came out of the One mind, and all things made by God came out of the same mind. Think prosperity thoughts. Think of riches of all kinds and the immense wealth of the world, and your subconscious will respond to your habitual thinking. Supplant all thoughts of poverty with the thought of God's opulence and endless resources. Be open and receptive, and let wealth flow freely to you. Be a good receiver.

3. **Your conscious mind is the pen with which you inscribe your true desires in your subconscious.** Think quietly and with interest of each desire separately, watering it and nurturing it with faith and expectancy. Do this three or four times a day. By frequent habitation of the mind, you will impregnate your subconscious, and the cherished desires of your heart will be realized.

4. Never engage in thinking of lack, limitation, loneliness and frustration. On the contrary, have a mental plan of the things you want, and then realize that whatever you attach to "I AM" you will create in your life. Get a little phrase easily graven on the memory, such as "I am happy, joyous, free," etc. Repeat it over and over again as a lullaby. Do it knowingly and feelingly. As you sow in your subconscious, so also will you reap.

5. Instead of grumbling, whining, and complaining about present conditions, reverse that attitude of mind and claim boldly: "Divine right action is mine. Divine success is mine. Divine love fills my soul, and whatever I do will prosper." Know that your

thoughts are creative and that you are what you think all day long. Have a healthy respect for your thoughts. Your *thought* is your *prayer.*

6. Begin to contemplate that God's beauty and riches flow freely through your thoughts, words and deeds and you will experience the results of your thinking; furthermore, you will be able to pass on to your family the riches acquired by contemplation. You must have in order to give. It is only the rich people who can contribute richly to all; the poor cannot give.

7. When you are in a quandary and are dealing with difficult people, it is a good thing to write out clearly your desire, as follows: "This, too, will pass away and there is a Divine and harmonious solution through the wisdom of my subconscious. I loose it and let it go now." You can put this written prayer in a drawer marked "With God all things are possible." This is a symbolic way of releasing it and it works wonders.

8. Life is a mirror for the king and the beggar, reflecting back to each of us precisely that which we deposit in our mind.

9. I have conducted group prayers on New Year's Eve where each person writes out his or her heart's desires. These prayers are sealed in an envelope, locked away for one year and opened the following New Year's Eve. Each member is amazed at the way their prayers were answered. Many had forgotten what they wrote and were astounded. The secret is that they released all their prayers with faith and confidence to the deeper mind, which knows all and sees all. They learned that when one has a Divine indifference, the prayer is always answered. Divine indifference is not carelessness or apathy; rather, it means that you know whatever you claim and feel to be true in your heart must

come to pass; therefore, you wait for the answer with greater faith, assurance and conviction than the man who waits for the coming of the dawn.

10. The meditation at the end of the chapter will yield you amazing benefits for daily living.

eight

How to Make and Use a Psychic Treasure Map

"The soul without imagination is what an observatory would be without a telescope."

H. W. Beecher

"Imagination disposes of everything; it creates beauty, justice, and happiness, which are everything in this world."

Pascal

"The poet's eye, in a fine frenzy rolling, doth glance from heaven to earth, from earth to heaven; and as imagination bodies forth the forms of things unknown, the poet's pen turns them to shape, and gives to airy nothing a local habitation and a name, such tricks had strong imagination."

Shakespeare

Imagination is one of our most powerful faculties. Disciplined, controlled, and directed imagination is a mighty instrument which plumbs the depths of your subconscious mind, bringing forth new inventions, discoveries, poems, music, and an awareness of the riches of the air, the sea and the earth. Scientists, artists, musicians, physicists, inventors, poets, and writers generally possess highly developed imaginative faculties, which draw forth from the treasure house of their subconscious the riches of the Infinite and bless mankind in countless ways.

How Her Treasure Map Brought
Her Riches and Companionship

Recently I performed a marriage ceremony for a young secretary who told me that about six months prior to her marriage, she drew up for herself a treasure map, dividing it into four parts: In the first section, she wrote, "I give thanks for God's wealth flowing freely in my life." In the second, she wrote, "I give thanks for a four-month trip around the world." In the third, she wrote, "I give thanks for a wonderful, spiritual-minded man who harmonizes with me perfectly." In the last, she wrote, "I give thanks for a wonderful home which is beautifully furnished." Underneath these four requests, she wrote, "I give thanks for the immediate fulfillment of all these requests in Divine order through Divine love."

Every morning, afternoon and evening, she would go over her requests, affirming and imagining their fulfillment, realizing that gradually these images would be written in her subconscious mind, which would bring them to pass. The answer to her first request came in about a month's time. Her grandmother in New York bequeathed $50,000 to her in her will and also her Cadillac car. Her mother and father, who are living in Canada, invited her to take a trip with them around the world, and on the trip she met a young scientist. As she said, it was love at first sight, and her marriage to him took place on her return to California. He had a beautiful home magnificently furnished.

She said to me that writing out a treasure map and trusting the infinite intelligence of her subconscious mind really works, and it does. In addition to the above technique, this young secretary got a passport, selected her tour and every night imagined she was on the plane visiting all the foreign countries. She also imagined a ring on her finger, which meant to her that she was already married to a wonderful man. In her imagination, she lived in a beautiful home surrounded by trees. And last but not least, she imagined going to her favorite teller in the bank and depositing $50,000, and he, in turn, congratulated her on her good fortune.

Her method helped her to get control over her thinking and imagination, enabling her to have dominion over her financial affairs, while at the same time bringing fulfillment in her love life and the field of expression.

His Imagination Brought About a Legal Settlement

On a visit to the ruins of Chichen Itza, famous for its pyramids and relics dealing with the ancient Mayan civilization, the guide informed me that Itza means "rattlesnake," and that the symbol was used throughout their culture.

Here I met an attorney from Texas, who happened to be staying at the same hotel, and he told me that after this vacation trip to the Mexican pyramids, he had a very tough assignment before him in Dallas, Texas, involving the settlement of conflicting claims among members of a family regarding a will involving about a million dollars. One member of the family had engaged him to bring peace and harmony so that a prolonged lawsuit could be avoided. He was quite apprehensive about it, since a settlement would render him a rather large fee.

I suggested that he practice the following imaginative form of prayer-therapy. Inasmuch as there is no time or space in the mental realm, he was to project himself mentally into a conference room in Dallas, where all the members of the family would be assembled, claiming harmony, peace and understanding to be operating among them. Accordingly, several times every day prior to his assignment, he imagined the member of the family who had hired him saying: "We have agreed to accept the terms of the will as written and will not contest it in court." He heard this over and over again and lulled himself to sleep every night with two words, "Happy ending."

Some weeks after I returned from the pyramids of Mexico, I had a letter from my attorney friend saying that he had followed my instructions, and at the family conference there was a complete agreement and a happy ending as well as a large check for the harmonious solution to what had threatened to be a rather nasty court battle between brothers and sisters.

How a Mexican Guide Uses His Imagination and Makes Extra Money

A guide who drove me to Uxmal, one of the major archaeological sites in Mexico which lies on the Merida-Compeche highway, slightly over an hour by motor car from the capital of the State of Yucatan, told me that during quiet periods when there are not so many tourists, his hobby is that of dowser and water diviner. He uses a bent piece of copper wire, and when he is asked to find water by a landowner, he visits the ranch, walks around and talks to his arm, saying to it, "You will get firm and rigid and the copper wire will point to the exact spot where water is." He added that in most instances he is correct. "The few times I fail," he said, "is due to the fact that I am too tired or that I don't concentrate enough."

He informed me that he had made enough extra money dowsing to enable him to get his degree from the university, and that in a short while he will become an instructor in archeology there. He showed me some maps also, which pinpointed where he had found lost cattle and lost sheep. He would study the map of the area and focus all his attention on the lost animal or animals and the wire would point to the exact spot.

He Was Simply Tapping the Riches Already in His Subconscious

When this young man was a very young boy, his father told him that he had inherited the gift of dowsing, and the young boy believed him. Inasmuch as the subconscious is amenable to suggestion and is controlled by suggestion, his subconscious responded according to his belief. Moreover, the subconscious mind is coextensive with all wisdom and intelligence, sees all and knows all; and it knows where water is, and where gold is, for the whole world came out of the universal subconscious.

Due to his belief and to his definite command to his subconscious mind, when he walks in an area where water is, his subconscious brings about a constriction of the muscles of his arm, a certain rigidity, and also acts on the wire, causing it to point to the spot to dig. I told him that he could improve his technique by suggesting frequently to his subconscious mind, "You will tell me exactly how many feet deep the water is" and "according to his belief is it done unto him."

The Law of Constructive Imagining
Overcame Her Discouragement

A widow came to me in a rather depressed, dejected and discouraged state. She had been trying to sell her two-story house for over a year. She had many people look at it, but none offered to buy, though they did not complain about the price. The upkeep was too much for her, and it was essential that she sell the home and retire to Leisure World, where an apartment was provided for her.

I outlined for her what she was to do in her imagination. She followed the instructions faithfully, and within three days her home was sold. At my suggestion, before going to sleep, she imagined a check in her hand for $100,000, the full price of the home. Then, in her controlled imagination, she deposited it in the bank with a great feeling of inner satisfaction. After this, and still in her imagination, she went into the apartment at Leisure World which she had visited several times, and which was being reserved for just a month based on her promise to take it.

In her drowsy sleep state, she slept on the divan of the apartment — all this in her imagination — and just before going off to sleep, she said, "Thank you, Father, for the fulfillment of my prayer in Divine order." She did this for three consecutive nights, and on the morning of the fourth day an executive from the East Coast saw the house and wanted to move in immediately. The price was right and everything else was right about it. He paid her cash in the form of a cashier's check for $100,000.

Truly, imagination has been called the workshop of God. Einstein said, "Imagination is greater than knowledge." What you can imagine and feel to be true will come to pass. Imagination clothes your ideas and projects them on the screen of space. Be faithful to that mental image in your mind and you will find that it will one day be projected on the screen of space.

How an Actress' Imagination Overcame Her Sense of Frustrating Competition

A beautiful actress who had been out of work for six months said to me that she had an opportunity for a wonderful part in a new movie, but that the producers were considering three others, also. Following their interview with her, she felt she could fit the part perfectly. I said to her that the idea of competition engenders anxiety, perhaps excess tension. I added that she might not get the part; therefore, I suggested that she do this: declare with faith and confidence, "I give thanks for my perfect expression at my highest level in Divine law and order. I accept my role in this movie or something grander, greater, or more wonderful, according to the riches of the Infinite, for me. It is God in action." Then I suggested she release the whole thing to her subconscious mind. Whenever the thought of the movie contract would come to her, she was to say, "Infinite Intelligence is taking care of that."

She did not receive the movie part she applied for, but shortly afterward she got a wonderful contract for overseas far more wonderful and exciting than the one she had desired originally. Whenever you are faced with what you believe to be competition for a job, assignment, or whatever, persist in the above simple procedure and get ready for the answer, which will come to you pressed down, shaken together, and running over.

The Rewards of Picturing Success and Riches

A few days ago, I had a lovely letter from a woman who, accompanied by her husband, is making a motion picture in France. Some years ago she had thought that everything was against her; everything seemed to go wrong in her life. I suggested to her, however, that she keep on imagining success and that the mental image, when repeated regularly, would overcome all her negativity; imagination is the most powerful faculty for success and riches when used in the right way.

Many times a day she would picture me in her mind's eye congratulating her on her wonderful success and marvelous achievements; also on her happy marriage. A few months later following an interview in my study, she left for England to visit her relatives. There she met and fell in love with a marvelous man who is thoroughly devoted to her. She got many television roles in England and now is engaged in a movie production in the south of France.

She wrote that it is true: whatever the mind expects, pictures and perseveres in comes to pass even though the evidence of the five senses seems to deny it. She dared to continue imagining her good, persevering every step of the way, proving that *the falling drops at last will wear the stone* (Lucretius). *Victory belongs to the most persevering* (Napoleon).

The Marvelous Power of a Master Image

Your dominant or master image controls all phases of your life. Your subconscious accepts the dominant of two ideas. (See *The Power of Your Subconscious Mind.*[1]) **A**

---

[1]See *The Power of Your Subconscious Mind* by Dr. Joseph Murphy, Prentice-Hall, Inc., Englewood Cliffs, N.J., 1963.

cigar salesman in downtown Los Angeles visited with me for an hour about five years ago. Today he is worth over half a million dollars. However, he was barely making ends meet five years ago. He lived in a trailer, had two boys, a wife, and an automobile that needed constant repair.

I explained to him how to use his imagination constructively, and he wrote down, at my suggestion: "I claim God's riches now, and my subconscious responds. I claim a beautiful home for my family. My wife, my two boys and I each need a car, and my subconscious brings these requests to pass. Promotion is mine. Success is mine. I give thanks for the fulfillment of all this now."

He and his wife made it a habit to mentally picture a lovely yard. They pictured a garage with four cars and a big bank account. Prior to sleep each night, he conveyed a message to his subconscious as follows: "I am ever grateful for God's riches, forever active, forever present, unchanging and eternal. I give thanks for my promotion and outstanding success."

Nothing happened for three months, then suddenly he was made manager of the store, and shortly thereafter his wife inherited property in Texas on which oil had been discovered. They moved to Texas where he now has the beautiful home, four cars and financial independence, since he is his own boss in charge of the oil wells worth over half a million dollars. It is written: "Whoever perseveres will be crowned" (Herden).

MEDITATION FOR EFFECTIVE IMAGINATION, THE WORKSHOP OF GOD FOR ALL GOOD

"'Where there is no vision, the people perish.' My vision is that I desire to know more of God and the way He works. My vision is for perfect health, harmony and peace. My vision is the inner faith that Infinite Spirit leads and guides me now in all ways. I know and believe that the God-Power within me answers my prayer; this is a deep conviction within me.

"I know that the mental picture to which I remain faithful will be developed in my subconscious mind and come forth on the screen of space.

"I make it my daily practice to imagine for myself and others only that which is noble, wonderful and God-like. I now imagine that I am doing the thing I long to do; I imagine that I now possess the things I long to possess; I imagine I am what I long to be. To make it real, I feel the reality of it; I know that it is so. Thank you, Father."

CHAPTER POINTS TO REMEMBER

1. The soul without imagination is what an observatory would be without a telescope. Imagination is the primal faculty of man, and it has the capacity to clothe your idea into visibility on the screen of space.

2. You can draw up for yourself a treasure map listing the cherished desires of your heart. Go over it several times a day, claiming and imaging the fulfillment of each desire now. Persevere and you will find that the images will be deposited in the subconscious, which will bring them to pass.

3. If you are apprehensive and worried about the outcome of a conference or legal controversy, quiet your mind and claim that harmony, peace and Divine understanding operate in the minds and hearts of all involved. Select the person who gave you the assignment and imagine he is telling you of the harmonious agreement and hear it over and over again. Lull yourself to sleep with "happy ending." You will succeed in impregnating the solution in your subconscious and there will be a Divine agreement.

4. A guide, believing that he inherited the capacity of dowsing, carried what he called a divining rod with him (copper wire), and he had convinced his subconscious mind that whenever he walked over

an area where water was, his arm would become rigid and the bent copper wire would point to the exact spot. His subconscious responded to his conviction, and he makes considerable money in this field of exploration.

5. If you have trouble selling a home, imagine you are holding the check for full payment in your hand prior to sleep; give thanks for the check, feel its reality, the naturalness and wonders of it all, and imagine yourself at the teller's window depositing the same amount. Give thanks to your Higher Self and you will find wonders happening as you pray that way.

6. When you are competing with others for a contract, assignment, position or role in the movies, avoid anxiety and tension by affirming, "I accept this assignment or something far more wonderful according to the riches of the Infinite for me." If you do not get that particular position, something far more wonderful will open up for you in the light of your Higher Self.

7. Even though your reason and senses deny the possibility of your attaining riches, promotion and success, persist in your master image for success, financial independence, a lovely home and the way you want things to be. Persist regularly and systematically, knowing that your master image will sink down into your subconscious mind and come to pass. One man earning only $100 a week five years ago proved that his persistent mental imagery caused him to fulfill all his dreams, including holdings of a half million dollars. This is the power of an overall master image. Whoever perseveres will be crowned.

8. Make full use of the meditation at the end of the chapter to help develop your greatest use of imagination for a richer life in every way.

nine

How the Law of Infinite Increase Multiplies Your Wealth

All men and women throughout the world are seeking to magnify their personal good. There is a Divine urge whispering to men and women everywhere to rise, transcend, grow and expand. It is an inner voice which says "Come on up higher. I have need of you."

You desire to have more of the worldly goods, a better position, friends, more money and luxuries of life. You desire the best food, clothing, the best automobile and all the other good things of life. Furthermore, you desire to travel all over the world and see the glories and beauties of this universe and the countless temples of beauty dedicated by man to God. Above all, you want to learn more about the riches-producing laws of your mind which will enable you to tap the treasure house of infinity within you and experience the life more abundant.

It is the nature of the soil to magnify and multiply the seeds you deposit in it. By depositing an acorn in the ground, you can in time look forward to a forest. *But God gave the increase* (I Corinthians 3:6). Likewise, when you plant the thoughts of riches, abundance, security and right action in your mind, and when you water them with faith and expectancy, riches and honor will be yours.

Increase means the multiplication of your good along all lines, spiritually, mentally, emotionally, socially and financially. Every thought is incipient action, and when you begin to think of the riches within your subconscious mind and all around you, you will be amazed how riches will flow to you from all sides.

In August, I conducted a seminar on the *Princess Italia,* which visited Canada and many ports in Alaska. In Victoria, Canada, eighteen students of the laws of mind visited me on the ship, and we discussed the wonders and wisdom of the subconscious for about three hours. Several of the men and women told me that in reading and applying the principles set forth in *The Power of Your Subconscious Mind,*[1] they had transformed their lives, experiencing a far greater measure of wealth, happiness, peace of mind and fullness of life.

How He Used the Law of Increase for Great Wealth

One man listening to our discussion on the subconscious mind on board the *Princess Italia* told me that years ago he was pondering over how poor he was. He also worried about the poverty and want he had observed in others. When he visited his relatives from time to time, he would come home and begin to talk about their financial lack and their poverty and sickness, always clothing them mentally in rags. He wondered why he never prospered either, even though he prayed that God would prosper him.

---

[1]See *The Power of Your Subconscious Mind* by Dr. Joseph Murphy, Prentice-Hall, Inc., Englewood Cliffs, N.J., 1963.

He visited a mind science counselor who told him that if he continued to think of others as living in poverty and lack and limitations of all kinds, due to the fact that every thought is creative, he was at the same time neutralizing his own prayer and impoverishing himself. It was, as he said, a great "eye-opener." He reversed his procedure and claimed that God was prospering him along all lines as well as every other person. He began to claim God's riches for every person he met, and he still does it!

Today he has two airplanes in Alaska for his private travel and is very successful in business and immensely wealthy. He learned a great fulfilling law: what you wish for another, you are wishing for yourself. There is an old Indian saying: "The ship that comes home to my brother comes home to me."

How a Professor Used the Law of Increase to His Personal Benefit

When I talked with a teacher on the above-mentioned cruise, he informed me that he attributed his success and advancement to professorship not only to his application to study, but also to the fact that he constantly, regularly and systematically made it a point to rejoice in the advancement, promotion and increments given his many associates in the college. He rejoiced and was exceedingly glad to see his associates go up the ladder, manifesting the law of increase and the riches of the Divine bounty which is omnipresent. He pointed out that it was several years later that he discovered that by appreciating and being happy about the good fortune of his co-workers he was at the same time promoting himself!

His thought and feeling entered into his subconscious mind, and whatever is deposited in the subconscious may come forth sixtyfold, a hundredfold, or even a thousandfold, depending on the enthusiasm, the joy and the intensity of the thought pattern. Today he is the youngest senior professor in his college. Rejoice in the idea of riches and ample supply for everyone, and you are certain to experience the law of increase in your own life.

How He Made a Dollar Increase in Important Wealth for Himself

During a conversation with an owner of a store in Juneau, Alaska, I learned that seven years ago he found himself in Juneau *with only one dollar in his pocket.* He said, "I looked at the silver dollar and began to talk to myself about everything in the world coming out either of the invisible mind of God or man; then I held the dollar in my hand and said over and over again for probably an hour: 'God multiplies this exceedingly, for it is God who giveth the increase.'"

Following this mental and spiritual exercise, he found a $100 bill on the street, which enabled him to check into a hotel and maintain himself for several days. He got a job in a restaurant, saved his money, took up flying lessons, and today one of his extra jobs is that of a bush pilot. From time to time he flies people all over Alaska, over glaciers, mountains and many scenic spots. He told me that in seven years he has amassed over a half million dollars in assets in conducting his unusual business.

He attributes all this to looking to the Source of all blessings and then boldly claiming that God's riches are flowing freely, joyously, endlessly and ceaselessly into his experience. His subconscious has responded to his mental attitude a thousandfold.

Perpetual Opportunity for Increase Exists for You

You can use the laws of your mind to advance, move forward and expand along all lines. Give the best where you are working now, i.e., be considerate, affable, amiable, loving, kind and full of goodwill to all those around you and to all people everywhere. Think big; contemplate the law of opulence and growth, evidence of which you perceive all around you. Bless what you are doing now, realizing that it is simply a stepping stone to your triumph and achievement. Recognize your true worth and claim wealth, promotion and recognition in your mind. Be sure to claim riches and expansion for every person you meet during the day, whether it be the boss, your associate, your customer or a friend. Make a habit of this, and you will succeed in impregnating your subconscious; moreover, others will feel your radiation of riches and promotion, and the law of attraction will open up new doors of opportunity for you.

How His Mental Picture Brought Advancement to Him

In 1970, I was a guest of a friend from Colombia while on a tour of Spain and Portugal. In Seville, I met a man at the Giralda Tower, which is the largest Gothic cathedral in the world, and which houses the remains of Christopher Columbus. This young man was twenty-seven years old, had come from Ecuador, and possessed an excellent command of the English language, as well as Spanish and Portuguese.

He pointed out a fascinating experience which had occurred about five years previously. A friend in Los Angeles had mailed him a copy of *The Power of Your Subconscious Mind.*[1] He had read it avidly and had followed one of the techniques written therein. He was finishing his university course at that time, and every night prior to sleep, he formed a mental picture of being a guide and conducting private groups to Spain and Portugal, knowing and believing that the power and wisdom of his subconscious would back him up. He had faith that the mental picture would be developed in his subconscious mind and be objectified.

The sequel was interesting. One of his professors asked him if he would conduct a very wealthy Canadian couple to Spain and Portugal and be their guide and interpreter, which

---

[1]See *The Power of Your Subconscious Mind,* by Dr. Joseph Murphy, Prentice-Hall, Inc. Englewood Cliffs, N.J., 1963.

offer he gladly accepted. His sojourn in Spain and Portugal has kept him busy acting as a private guide, chauffeur and interpreter for their many wealthy friends. All his expenses are paid and he nets the equivalent of about $10,000 a year, which is exceptionally good for a young man in Spain or Portugal.

He knew what he was doing and why he was doing it. Undoubtedly, the subtle law of attraction brought both of us together, since I was seeking material to write about on the trip. There is nothing in all the world to restrain, restrict or inhibit your advancement on the road to riches but yourself, i.e., your own thought and concept of yourself. When you are seeking and imaging promotion, true expression, increased status and prestige, believe in the powers of your deeper mind to bring it to pass, and you will enter into the advancing life and experience the riches of God here and now.

Why the Law of Increase Did Not Work for Him

A businessman complained to me that he had been affirming prosperity, abundance and success but was getting no results. In talking with him, I discovered that he was actually boasting about his financial embarrassment; moreover, he was blaming the government, the taxes, welfare and the whole political system. He believed he was a victim of conditions and circumstances instead of master of the situation.

When I explained the laws of mind to him, he perceived that as long as he was complaining and harping on his financial troubles, he would only magnify them and continue to impoverish himself, inasmuch as what he gives attention to in his subconscious multiplies.

How He Reversed His Faulty Thinking

At my suggestion, he reversed his thinking process and began to realize that he could begin to practice a creative process of thinking which would transcend circumstances and environmental conditions. His daily prayer was as follows:

"My business is God's business, and God's business always prospers. I use God's riches wisely, judiciously and constructively to bless myself and others. I know the law of increase is now working and I am open and receptive to God's wealth and bountiful increase. I am richly and abundantly supplied within and without from the infinite storehouse of riches in my subconscious mind. By day and by night I am attracting more and more people who want what I have to offer. They are prospered and I am prospered. My mind and heart are open to the influx of God's riches now and forevermore."

As he fed his mind with these inner truths, his business prospered and his outer supply became more abundant. At the end of a month, he noticed a tremendous change in his financial picture. He saw the great advantage in affirming the good and in ceasing to carp against lack and limitation. He discovered that attention to God's riches is the key to financial success.

The Significance of the Statement "My Cup Runneth Over" in the 23rd Psalm

My Colombian friend and I stopped for lunch at the internationally known shrine of Fatima, and we had no sooner sat down than a young girl from Alabama came over to our table and introduced herself, saying: "Dr. Murphy, thank you for your letter and prayer you sent me last year. I followed the instructions and here I am."

I had no recollection of the letter, and she explained that she had written saying that she wanted to go to the Shrine of Fatima but that she didn't have the money, and she had asked me how to pray. I gathered from her conversation that this high school girl had read the story of Fatima and had an intense desire to go to the shrine, but her parents, being very poor, could not afford it.

She had a copy of the prayer I had given her: "God opens up the way for me to go to the Shrine of Fatima during the summer in Divine order through Divine love." I also suggested that every night, with her physical body immobilized, she imagine herself as getting off the plane at Lisbon, opening her baggage, showing her passport to the Portuguese officials, and feel that she is actually in her imagination at the shrine, entering the church, and hearing and seeing all that she would see and hear and do if she were physically there. I pointed out to her that she was to lull herself to sleep every night dramatizing the picture until she felt the naturalness and the reality of it all, and that when she felt at peace about it, the way would be opened up.

She said that at the end of about two weeks following the prayer process, she had no further desire to pray about it because, obviously, she had succeeded in fixing the state in her subconscious mind. She was invited to spend a weekend at a girl friend's home whose father was taking a trip to Portugal and Spain in 1970 and who intended to visit the shrine also. She was invited to come along as their guest, and she accepted with alacrity.

The Bible says: *I go to prepare a place for you. And if I go and prepare a place for you, I will come again, and receive you unto myself; that where I am, there ye may be also.* (John 14:2,3)

This high school girl prepared the place she wanted to go in her disciplined imagination, and the moment came when she felt at peace about it, knowing she had succeeded in impregnating her subconscious with the picture, because she no longer had any desire to pray about it. Then her subconscious took over and acted on the mind of her friend's father, and he became the channel for the answer to her prayer.

She said to me: *My cup runneth over* (Psalm 23:5).

It is written: *Ask, and it shall be given you* (Matthew 7:7).

MEDITATION FOR YOUR BUSINESS
OR PROFESSIONAL SUCCESS

Use the following powerful meditation to fill your cup of success in all things:

"I now dwell on the Omnipresence and Omniaction of God. I know that this Infinite Wisdom guides the planets on their courses. I know this same Divine Intelligence governs and directs all my affairs. I claim and believe Divine understanding is mine at all times. I know that all my activities are controlled by this indwelling Presence. All my motives are God-like and true. God's wisdom, truth and beauty are being expressed by me at all times. The All-Knowing One within me knows what to do, and how to do it. My business or profession is completely controlled, governed and directed by the love of God. Divine guidance is mine. I know God's answer, for my mind is at peace. I rest in the Everlasting Arms."

CHAPTER POINTS TO REMEMBER

1. Increase is what all people throughout the world are seeking; it is the Divine urge within us seeking fuller, greater, grander expression in all phases of our lives. You plant wheat, barley or oats in the soil, but it is God who giveth the increase by multiplying the wheat grains a thousandfold.

2. Increase means the multiplication of your good along all levels.

3. Do not talk about the financial lack, poverty or sickness of others. To do so is to attract more lack to yourself. Clothe everybody mentally with the riches of God. Cease thinking of your own financial troubles and stop talking about your lack of money. Give attention to the riches of the Infinite within and without, and you will prosper. Attention is the key to life.

4. Rejoice in the advancement, good fortune, riches and promotion of all those around you. Be exceedingly glad to see people experience, portray and demonstrate the riches of God, and as you do, you will attract riches of all kinds to yourself. Your thought is creative, and what you think about the other, you are creating in your own experience.

5. Be friendly with money, whether a dollar bill or a coin. Realize everything comes out of the invisible mind of God or of man. Realize that God, or Infinite Spirit, is the Source of all blessings and that it is the nature of the Infinite to respond when you call upon it. One man had only a dollar left, and for over an hour he affirmed: "God multiplies this exceedingly, for it is God who giveth the increase." His subconscious opened up all doors for him, and in a short time he became a fabulous success and amassed a fortune.

6. Give the best where you are working and the best will come back to you. Be friendly, affable, amiable and express goodwill to all. As you do, all doors will open up for your growth, expansion and riches.

7. Form a clear mental picture of what you want to be, to do or to have; know that the power and the wisdom of your subconscious will back you up. Persevere and be determined what you want to be. Your mental picture will be developed in your subconscious mind and become objectified.

8. When you are praying for increase in money, be sure to stop blaming the government, the welfare system and taxes. To do so will cause money to fly from you rather than to you. What you want is more money. Realize that God's wealth is circulating in your life and that there is always a Divine surplus. What you criticize and condemn becomes manifest in your life. You become what you contemplate. Contemplate that God multiplies

your good exceedingly and that your business is God's business and that you are prospering beyond your fondest dreams.

9. If you want to take a trip around the world or to any particular place, and if you don't have a sou in your pocket, affirm knowingly and feelingly: "God opens up the way for me to go around the world in Divine order and through Divine love." Picture yourself with a passport on the plane or ship, visiting all the key spots in the world. Enter into the reality of it in your imagination until you feel the tones of reality. As soon as you fix the picture in your subconscious, the way will open up, the dawn will appear and all the shadows will flee away. *Ask, and it shall be given you* (Matthew 7:7).

10. The meditation at the end of the chapter will be of exceptional benefit to you in filling your cup of successful living.

ten

How to Open the Gateway to Automatic Riches and Walk into a Life of Luxury

The gateway to infinite riches is hidden in that magic spiritual gem given to you in the Bible: *I am come that they might have life, and that they might have it more abundantly* (John 10:10).

Down through the ages, man has been seeking the key to riches and success, yet not knowing that the key was within himself.

You are here to lead a full and happy life, to give expression to your hidden talents and release the imprisoned splendor within you. God is the giver and the gift, and all the riches of God are awaiting your discovery, application and enjoyment.

By applying the laws of your mind, you can draw forth from the treasure house within you everything you need in order to lead a rich, glorious, abundant and satisfactory life.

How She Opened the Gateway to Riches for Herself

A few years ago, I gave a class on Mental and Spiritual Laws in the Light of Emerson, and there was a young woman present who had that morning gone to a relief agency for financial help for herself and two children. Her husband had walked out and simply disappeared. She listened as I quoted from Emerson and elaborated in light of the laws of mind. Emerson said: "In all my lectures, I have taught one doctrine — the infinitude of the private man, the ever-availability to every man of the Divine presence within his own mind, from which presence he draws, at his need, inexhaustible power."

This statement of Emerson made a profound impression on her because she saw it in a new light. She had studied Emerson in college but just as literature and, as she said, got nothing out of it. The following is the prayer she uttered to draw from the Divine presence within her.

How She Demonstrated Money

Several times a day, she declared with feeling, enthusiasm and understanding, "I recognize the Source within and I make contact with my thought, and I do give thanks that the gateway to riches is now open wide for me, and God's riches are flowing freely to me, and more and more money is circulating in my life every day. Every day of my life I am growing richer spiritually, mentally, financially and in all ways. Money is God's idea circulating in my life, and there is always a surplus." *The living God, who giveth us richly all things to enjoy* (I Timothy 6:17).

She began to realize that according to her inner thought life, so would her exterior life be. Emerson said, "The key to every man is his thought." As she continued meditating faithfully, boldly, deliberately and decisively on money, financial security and prosperity along all lines, after the lapse of about three weeks she received a notice from an attorney in Houston that her grandfather, who had passed on, had bequeathed one of his very productive oil wells to her and that she was to begin to receive revenue from it immediately. All her financial troubles were settled legally and the true value of the oil well will probably run into the millions. She discovered that the gateway to millions was through her own subconscious mind. Its ways are past finding out.

How He Found the Gateway to True Expression

A while ago, I interviewed a man who was dismissed by the new owner of the organization with which he had been associated for thirty years. He said to me that everywhere he applied he had been turned down because of his age. I explained to him that he was not selling his age but the knowledge, experience and wisdom he had garnered through the years, and that what he was seeking was really seeking him. Each night and morning he prayed, knowing that his subconscious mind was the gateway to expression, abundance and the riches of life. His prayer was as follows:

"Infinite Intelligence knows my hidden talents and opens up a new door of expression for me in Divine order. This knowledge is immediately revealed to my conscious mind, and I will follow the lead which comes clearly and definitely into my mind."

At the end of a week, he met an old friend in his club, who said to him, "Tom, there is a place in our organization for you. I think you are the man for it." He accepted the offer at once, which proved to be far more remunerative than his previous position.

Remember, it is from within, not from without, that you get in touch with the riches of life. Radio and TV programs permeate your environment, but you must dial the right channel or radio station to get what you want.

How a Trip to Japan Became a Reality

One of my Japanese listeners to my morning radio program told me how she arranged to spend three months in Japan this year. She said that I had pointed out one morning that if you want to take a trip and do not have a penny in your pocket that you were to believe you have received the answer and to take some action that would indicate you had faith that your prayer was already answered in your deeper mind, i.e., to adopt the mental attitude of being already in the country or on the plane, having your passport and bags ready and all other requirements needed for overseas travel.

This girl got a passport, vaccination shots, travel folders to Japan, and imagined she was embracing and kissing her grandmother in Tokyo and conducting a vigorous conversation in Japanese with her. She dramatized this role over and over again each night until she felt the naturalness of it all plus the sensory vividness of embracing her grandmother and hearing her voice.

Shortly after this prayer process, she met a young attorney, and this author had the joy of performing the wedding ceremony. The groom took his bride to Japan for a three-month honeymoon, and she experienced a lovely visit with her grandmother. The wisdom of her subconscious not only answered her prayer, but magnified her good in bringing love and romance into her life. Your subconscious always gives you compound interest. Your good can come forth to you in unforeseen ways.

A Physicist Says Substance Is the Gateway to All the Money You Need

A young physicist visited me recently and he pointed out that Einstein and all our modern physicists realize that Spirit and matter are one, and that energy and matter are interconvertible and interchangeable; that matter is the lowest degree of Spirit and that Spirit is the highest degree of matter. In other words, they are one and the same thing. Further, that matter is, then, universal *substance,* or Spirit, or Energy reduced to the point of visibility. *The formed and unformed world are made out of the one substance which we call Spirit.* All things are made by the self-contemplation of Spirit.

He said to me, "When I came to America, all I had was ten dollars, but I didn't get panicky, as I knew the invisible would become visible, and I declared in my hotel room, 'Divine Spirit is my instant and everlasting supply. It takes the form of food, clothing, money, friends and everything I need right here and right now. I decree this and I know the manifestation takes place now, for God is the Eternal Now!'"

His good came to him through a *total stranger,* whom he met in the hotel elevator. As they conducted a vigorous conversation in French, though both spoke excellent English, the stranger arranged for him to get a position with an electronic research organization. He has been promoted and is now a partner in the organization.

Never underestimate the powers of personally affirming God, or the Living Spirit Almighty, your instant and everlasting supply which never fails. It will then manifest in countless ways and through many channels; perhaps through total strangers. Remember, you were born to be rich and inevitably to prosper along all lines through the use of your God-given faculties which lie stretched in smiling repose within you.

How to Help Others to the Gateway
of Riches, True Place and Honor

When you wish to help a friend, a relative, an associate or anyone who seeks your help to find his or her true place in life and become rich in livingness and givingness, use the following prayerful meditation in activating the forces for them:

"Infinite Spirit in Its wisdom opens up the gateway for So-and-so's true expression in life, where he is doing what he loves to do, is Divinely happy and Divinely prospered. He is Divinely led to the right people, who appreciate his talents, and he receives marvelous and wonderful income for wonderful service. He is conscious of his true worth and he is blessed and prospered with God's riches beyond his fondest dreams. I turn this prayer over to my subconscious mind, which has the know-how of accomplishment and it brings it to pass in Divine order."

Repeat the above prayer slowly, quietly, feelingly and knowingly, pouring life, love, and enthusiasm into your words, and you will be amazed how the wisdom of the subconscious will respond. It never fails.

His Attitude Closed the Gateway to His Riches

Recently, during a lecture series in San Diego, a man came to see me in the hotel. He had been praying morning and night for prosperity and promotion. He was well-educated and was working for the government but had not received any increment or promotion in several years, and to make matters worse, he had lost heavily on the stock market, particularly on silver futures. He said, "I'm wiped out." In talking to him, I discovered he held deep-seated grudges and prejudices against former employers as well as his present superiors in his department.

I explained to him that his mind cluttered up with hostility, grudges and peeves plus a failure attitude neutralized all his prayers, somewhat like mixing an acid and an alkali, one neutralizing the other.

I suggested he redirect his mind and emphasize prosperous thinking and enter into the spirit of forgiveness for himself and others. Accordingly, he began to practice the following technique of prayer: "I forgive myself for harboring negative and destructive thoughts, and I release my former employers and present associates to God completely, wishing for them all the blessings of life. Whenever I think of any one of them, I will immediately affirm, 'I have released you; God be with you.' I know as I continue to do this, that I will meet them in my mind and that there will be no longer any sting present. I claim promotion now, success now, harmony now. Divine law and order is mine now. God's wealth flows to me in avalanches of abundance. Life is growth and expansion, and I am an open channel for God's riches, which are ever-active, ever-present, unchanging and eternal. I give thanks now for the riches within and without, and what I am now decreeing shall come to pass and the light of God shall shine on me."

Following this prayer process several times a day, and making sure he did not subsequently deny what he affirmed earlier in the day, he found himself attracting new people and being "led" to certain books, certain teachers and to classes on the subconscious mind. He discovered that he had set into operation certain subtle forces of his subconscious mind which correlated with his habitual thinking and prayer life. He was promoted with much higher pay to the Los Angeles office. He discovered that his changed attitude was really the gateway to fulfillment of his dreams. Dream noble and God-like dreams, and as you dream, so shall you become. You go where your vision is.

MEDITATION FOR OPENING THE
GATEWAY TO RIGHT ACTION

The following meditation will establish judgment and confidence in taking the right action for any situation:

"I radiate goodwill to all mankind in thought, word and deed. I know the peace and goodwill that I radiate to every man comes back to me a thousandfold. Whatever I need to know comes to me from the God-Self within me. Infinite Intelligence is operating through me revealing to me what I need to know. God in me knows only the answer. The perfect answer is made known to me now. Infinite Intelligence and Divine Wisdom make all decisions through me, and there is only right action and right expression taking place in my life. Every night I wrap myself in the Mantle of God's Love and fall asleep knowing Divine Guidance is mine. When the dawn comes, I am filled with peace. I go forth into the new day full of faith, confidence and trust. Thank you, Father."

CHAPTER POINTS TO REMEMBER

1. The gateway to infinite riches is based on the spiritual gem: *I am come that they might have life, and that they might have it more abundantly* (John 10:10). You are here to lead a full, happy and rich life. You are here to squeeze the last drop of happiness out of life.

2. Emerson taught one doctrine — the infinitude of the private man. This means that the riches of the Infinite are within you. This also means that you can contact all the powers of the God-head in you through your thought life, and as you think of riches, guidance, inspiration, and creative ideas, there will be a response according to the nature of your thought. It responds by corresponding.

3. You are not selling your age to employers but your talents, abilities, wisdom and experience garnered through the years. Realize that what you are seeking is also seeking you and claim that Infinite Spirit is opening up a new door of expression for you where you are amply rewarded financially, and It will respond accordingly. It never fails.

4. If you want to take a trip anywhere around the world or to any specific foreign country, act as though your prayer were answered and do all the things you would do to prepare for the trip as if you actually had the money in your pocket. "Believe you have it now and you shall receive it." You can order a passport or identification card and in your imagination feel yourself in that country or city now. Repeat the drama frequently until it gets into your subconscious, and then it will come to pass.

5. Spirit and matter are one. Energy and matter are one. The scientist uses the term energy for Spirit, which is God. God is the only presence, power,

cause and substance; therefore, Spirit is the reality of money, food, clothing, the grass and the field, and all the metals; and the whole world of matter is simply Spirit in form, or reduced to the point of visibility. Claim that God or Spirit is your instant and everlasting supply and that money is now flowing to you freely, joyously and endlessly this very moment. Believe and know, realize and understand that the formless is forever taking form. Let money and all kinds of riches flow to you now.

6. When you wish to pray for riches and true expression for another, realize that Infinite Spirit opens up the gateway for his true expression and that God's riches are flowing to him in avalanches of abundance.

7. Changed attitudes change everything. If a man will place emphasis on the spirit of forgiveness and goodwill to all and also forgive himself for harboring thoughts of failure, lack and resentment, and then pour life, love, energy and vitality into his thoughts of promotion, riches, expansion, honor, prestige and recognition, his deeper mind will respond with compound interest, and his desert will rejoice and blossom as the rose.

8. Allow the meditation at the end of the chapter to penetrate your thinking for deciding on right action to take.

eleven

How to Choose Your Wealth Goals and Receive Them Right Away

The Bible gives us the answer: *Choose you this day whom ye will serve* (Joshua 24:15).

The key to your health, wealth, prosperity and success in life lies in your wonderful capacity to make decisions. The greatest discovery you can make is to awaken to the great truth that there is an infinite wisdom and power already established within you, enabling you to solve all your problems, and to become wealthy, happy, joyous and free. You were born to win and you are equipped with all the powers of God within you to make you master of your fate and captain of your destiny.

If you are not aware of your capacity to choose from the Kingdom of Heaven within you, which is the presence of God lodged in your deeper mind, you will begin to choose and make decisions based on events, circumstances and conditions around you. What is worse, you will tend to overlook the powers within you and will exalt the powers of circumstance which may exist at a certain time. Choose from the Kingdom of God within you, and move forward on the high road to happiness, health, freedom and the joy of living the abundant life.

The Power of Choice

Your power to choose is your most distinctive quality and your highest prerogative. Your capacity to choose and to initiate what is chosen reveals your power to create as a son of God.

How His Power to Choose Transformed His Life

An alcoholic, by which I mean a compulsive drinker, visited me a few months ago. I explained to him that he had the God-given capacity to choose sobriety, peace of mind, happiness and prosperity right here and right now. He was sincere in his desire to become free from what he called his "curse."

The following prayer was given to him: "I choose health, peace of mind, freedom and sobriety right now. This is my decision. I know that the Almighty Power backs up my choice. I am relaxed, and God's river of peace flows through me. My spiritual food and drink are God's ideas and eternal verities, which unfold within me bringing me harmony, health, peace and joy. In my imagination I am back with my family, doing what I love to do and am Divinely happy. Whenever the urge to drink comes, I flash this mental movie in my mind and the God Power backs me up."

He repeated this prayer four or five times a day, while being aware that he was writing these thoughts in his subconscious mind, which accepts repeated thought patterns affirmed convincingly and decisively. The shakes and the jitters still came occasionally, but he flashed on the screen of his mind the mental movie and vision of himself at home with his wife and family and working at his former profession. His desire to give up the bad habit was greater than his desire to continue it, and the power of his subconscious backed him up.

The Riches of the Right Choice for Everyone

Every morning when you awake, choose the following eternal truths, remembering that your lifetime experiences, conditions and circumstances are the sum total of your choice. Affirm boldly as follows: "Today is God's day. I choose harmony, peace, perfect health, Divine law and order, Divine love, beauty, abundance, security and inspiration from On High. I know as I claim these truths in my life, that I awaken and activate the powers of my subconscious which compel me to express all these powers and qualities. I know it is as easy for God to become all these things in my life as it is to become a blade of grass. I give thanks that this is so."

The above should be the choice of every person every day. These are principles of life, and as you affirm them, you make all these powers of God active and potent in your life. Your subconscious accepts what you consciously believe, and it is easy for you to believe in the principles of harmony, peace, beauty, love, joy and abundance.

Emerson said: "Nothing can bring you peace but the triumph of principles." There is a principle of beauty, but none of ugliness; there is a principle of harmony, but none of discord; there is a principle of love, none of hatred; there is a principle of joy, none of sadness; there is a principle of opulence and abundance, none of deprivation and poverty; and there is a principle of right action, none of wrong action. Begin to choose what is true of God and His goodness and the riches of life will be yours.

Decide to Choose the Riches
of the Divinity Within You

People who are afraid to make choices are actually refusing to recognize their own Divinity, for God indwells all men. It is your Divine right to make choices based on eternal verities, and the great principles of life, which never change. Choose to be healthy, happy, prosperous, and successful, because you have dominion over your world of finance, business, health, profession and relationships with others. Your subconscious mind is subject to the decrees and convictions of your conscious mind, and whatever you decree convincingly shall come to pass.

The Bible says: *Whatsoever a man soweth, that shall he also reap* (Galatians 6:7).

What Happens on Failing to Choose?

A woman said to me, "I don't know what to choose or what is reasonable or logical." I explained to her that she had made a choice; she had chosen not to choose, which meant that she had chosen to take what comes from the mass mind or the law of averages, in which we are all immersed. Also, if she had chosen not to choose, the random or irrational mind of the multitude would choose for her, inasmuch as she refused to choose for herself.

She began to perceive that it was very foolish for her not to choose thoughts, images and ideals for herself; that she was here to do her own thinking, reasoning and choosing; otherwise, the mind of the masses would do her choosing for her and manipulate her mind along undesirable lines.

She reversed her attitude, however, and asserted constructively: "I am a choosing, volitional being. I have the power, the ability and the wisdom to control and to direct my own mental and spiritual processes. I say to myself every morning when I awaken: 'God indwells me. What am I going to choose today from the treasure house of infinity within me? I choose peace, Divine guidance, right action in my life, and decree that *goodness, truth and mercy shall follow me all the days of my life: and I will dwell in the house of the Lord forever* (Psalm 23:6).'"

Following this manner of choice, this woman has transformed her life. She has better health, increased efficiency, more understanding and has prospered along all lines.

The Infinite Power Backs Up Your Choices

You are a self-conscious individual and, as you know, you have the capacity to choose. After deliberation, you select one suit of clothes in preference to another; in like manner, you choose your minister, doctor, dentist, home, wife, husband, food, and car. In other words, you are constantly being called upon to choose in this three-dimensional plane. What kind of thoughts and images are you choosing? I want to reiterate and emphasize again that your whole life represents the sum total of your choices. Choose wisely, judiciously and constructively. Choose the truths of God which never change. They are the same yesterday, today and forever.

Some say, "I will let God choose for me." When you say that, you mean a God outside yourself. God, or the Living Spirit, is omnipresent and is also within you, the very life of you. The only way God, or Infinite Intelligence, will work for you is through you. In order for the Universal to act on the individual plane, It must become the individual.

You are here to choose. You have volition and initiative. This is why you are an individual. Accept your Divinity and your responsibility and choose for yourself, make decisions for yourself; the other person or your relative does not know best. When you refuse to choose for yourself, you are actually rejecting your Divinity and your Divine prerogatives and you are thinking from the standpoint of a slave, a serf and an underling.

Her Courage to Choose Transformed and Enriched Her Life

A widow came to me perplexed, baffled and frustrated because she had a choice to make between two men and could not make up her mind which one to marry. I told her an old story about the donkey placed at a central point between two stacks of hay, and he starved to death because he could not make a choice as to which one was his food for the day.

I suggested that she had the capacity and ability to choose Infinite Intelligence within her to lead and guide her, and that Its nature was responsiveness. I advised her that the answer would come to her clearly and that it would be impossible for her to miss it.

Accordingly, on going to sleep that night, she spoke as follows to her Higher Self: "Father, you are All-Wise. Reveal to me the answer and show me the way I should go. I give thanks for the right answer, for I know You know only the answer." She had a dream that night in which both of the above-mentioned men said, "Goodbye" to her. Then a third man, her employer, appeared in the dream and asked her to marry him. She knew the answer when she awoke, and the very next day her boss asked her to marry him, which offer she accepted.

She followed the Biblical injunction, *Choose you this day whom ye will serve* (Joshua 24:15). Turn to the Infinite Intelligence within you and call upon It, and you will receive the joy of the answered prayer. You can choose confidence, riches and a full life. Many say that they have always experienced sickness, failure, frustration and loneliness. All these failures can be dissolved by choosing to believe in the One Infinite Healing Presence. Feeling and emotion follow thought. You can, therefore, choose to build a new emotional life. Recognize that the will of God for you is the tendency of the Life-Principle Itself, which seeks to flow through you as harmony, health, peace, joy, creative ideas, and prosperity, extending beyond your fondest dreams. You have chosen to believe that what is true of God is true of you; therefore, from this moment forward, the preponderance of your thought and expectancy will come from Him who giveth to all life, breath and all things. In other words, your mind and heart will be always open for the influx of God's riches now and forevermore.

MEDITATION FOR BUILDING YOUR ACCOUNT AT YOUR PROSPERITY BANK

"I know that my good is this very moment. I believe in my heart that I can prophesy for myself harmony, health, peace and joy. I enthrone the concept of peace, success and prosperity in my mind now. I know and believe these thoughts (seeds) will grow and manifest themselves in my experience.

"I am the gardener; as I sow, so shall I reap. I sow God-like thoughts (seeds); these wonderful seeds are peace, success, harmony and goodwill. It is a wonderful harvest.

"From this moment forward I am depositing in the Universal Bank (my subconscious mind) seeds or thoughts of peace, confidence, poise and balance. I am drawing out the fruit of the wonderful seeds I am depositing. I believe and accept the fact that my desire is a seed deposited in the subconscious. I make it real by feeling the reality of it. I accept the reality of my desire in the same manner I accept the fact that the seed deposited in the ground will grow. I know it grows in the darkness; also, my desire or ideal grows in the darkness of my subconscious mind; in a little while, like the seed, it comes above the ground (becomes objectified) as a condition, circumstance or event.

"Infinite Intelligence governs and guides me in all ways. I meditate on whatsoever things are true, honest, just, lovely and of good report. I think on these things, and God's Power is with my thoughts of Good. I am at peace."

CHAPTER POINTS TO REMEMBER

1. The key to your health, wealth, prosperity and success lies in your capacity to choose. Choose whatsoever things are true, lovely, noble and God-like. Choose thoughts, ideas and images which heal, bless, inspire, dignify and elevate your whole being.

2. Your power to choose is your highest prerogative, enabling you to select from the infinite treasure house within you all the blessings of life.

3. When an alcoholic chooses to select harmony, peace, sobriety and right action in his life, knowing the Almighty Power will back up his choice, he is on the way to release from his habit, and to free-

dom and perfect health. He uses the wonderful power of disciplined imagination in realizing that he is doing what he loves to do, dramatizing the mental movie over and over again until it has all the tones of reality. The minute the idea of freedom is fixed in his subconscious mind, he is compelled to freedom and sobriety.

4. A wonderful choice for everyone every morning of your life is to affirm: "Divine right action is mine. Divine law and order govern my life. Divine peace is mine. Divine love fills my soul. Divine harmony reigns supreme. Divine beauty fills my soul. I am inspired and Divinely led in all ways. There is a happy outcome to all my undertakings." Make a habit of this and wonders will happen in your life.

5. Never hesitate to make a choice. You are a volitional, choosing being, and to refuse to choose is actually to reject your own Divinity. You can choose according to universal truths and principles of God, which never change.

6. In failing to choose for yourself, you are actually saying that you are going to let the mass mind, full of irrational fears, superstitions and ignorance of all kinds, make choices for you. If you do not choose to do your own thinking, the mass mind and the propaganda of the world will make choices for you. There is no such thing as indecision. It simply means you have decided not to decide. Don't let Tom, Dick and Harry make up your mind. Choose God and His Truth.

7. Choose that goodness, truth and beauty will follow you all the days of your life because you dwell in the house of God forever.

8. Your whole life consists of a series of choices. All of your experiences are the sum total of your choices. You are always choosing your books, clothes, schools, partners, homes, automobiles, and so on.

Watch the kind of thoughts, images and ideas you choose. You are what you think all day long. Choose what is lovely and of good report.

9. God, or Infinite Intelligence, will do nothing for you except through your thought, images and choices. The Universal cannot act on the individual except It becomes the individual.

10. Choose God and realize that only God knows the answer. If perplexed and wondering how to choose between two suitors, realize God, or Infinite Intelligence, knows the answer. Contemplate the answer and the Supreme Intelligence will respond accordingly. It never fails.

11. Regardless of past errors, sickness and failures, believe now the absolute truth that the will of God for you is a greater measure of life, love, truth, and beauty, transcending your fondest dreams. Open your mind and heart and live in the joyous expectancy of the life more abundant now and forevermore!

12. Use the meditation at the end of the chapter to build up your account in the Prosperity Bank.

twelve

How to Hear the Gentle, Invisible Voices That Can Guide You to Wealth

Your subconscious mind seeks to protect you at all times. Therefore, you should learn to listen to the inner promptings of intuition. Your subjective self governs all your vital organs and will continue to maintain them in equilibrium and balance unless your conscious mind intrudes with worry, anxiety, fears and negative thoughts. These negative thoughts upset the Divine norm within your deeper mind. Within your subconscious mind is the Divine Presence, which you can call your Higher Self, the Superconscious, the I AM, or "The Christ in you, the hope of Glory." All these terms mean the same thing.

Your subconscious mind reacts to suggestion and the commands of your conscious mind. You can, therefore, train your conscious mind to recognize the promptings of your subjective mind in the right direction. Usually, when you are relaxed and your mind is at peace, your conscious mind is more closely *en rapport* with your subconscious mind, and then the inner voice of intuition is heard and felt clearly and distinctly.

She Was Glad She Listened to
That Inner Voice

Mrs. Jean Wright, who is my secretary, told me that some years ago she and her mother planned to go away for a weekend, but on Saturday she had that inner feeling, a deep-seated "hunch," which seemed to say, "Stay at home." It was a persistent feeling, which she obeyed. It developed that her son had a serious accident at the beach later that day, and she was able to get him to a dental surgeon immediately, who rectified the condition at once. The dental surgeon was just leaving his home on a trip the moment she called. The inner prompting was correct in every way.

How to Follow and Recognize the
Voice of Intuition

The best guide is the knowledge which comes from the correct instructions to your subconscious mind, which will enable you to distinguish the true from the false. When you have a sincere desire for the truth, knowing that Infinite Spirit responds according to the nature of your thought, you will get results.

Use the following prayer frequently: "Infinite Intelligence is my constant guide and counselor. I will instantly recognize the promptings and monitions that come from my Higher Self, which forever seek to protect, guide, and watch over me in all ways. I will instantly recognize the 'lead' which comes into my conscious mind, and I will always disregard groundless fancies. I know that my deeper mind responds to what I am now consciously writing on it, and I give thanks for the joy of the answered prayer."

As you make a habit of using this prayer and of praying as a habit, you will be able to instantly recognize the interior voice by an inward sense of touch enabling you to differentiate and distinguish between the false and the true.

How Cultivation of the Intuitive Faculty
Brings Riches to You

You will receive answers and directions from your subconscious mind based on what you consciously meditate upon. The question you entertain or turn over to your deeper mind gestates in the darkness of your subconscious, and when all the data are gathered, you receive instantaneously that which your intellect, or reasoning mind, could accomplish only after weeks of monumental trial and error. When our reasoning faculties fail us in our perplexities, the intuitive faculty sings the silent song of triumph.

Artists, poets, writers and inventors listen to this voice of intuition. As a result, they are able to astonish the world by the beauties and glories drawn from this storehouse of knowledge within themselves. They have discovered the source of true riches.

The Infinite Riches of Intuition Saved His Life

Many of you may have read about the recent Japanese air disaster where so many unfortunate people lost their lives. I received a letter from a Japanese student who had been reading *The Power of Your Subconscious Mind.*[1] He stated that he was scheduled to fly on that plane, but that on the way to the airport, he had heard an inner voice saying clearly to him, "Don't go on that plane," a voice whose texture, sound and substance he heard as plainly as the voice over a radio. He cancelled the trip. This student has trained his mind to watch over him in all his ways.

Intuition and What It Means

Intuition means the direct perception of truth, independent of any reasoning process, immediate apprehension, a keen and quick insight. The word "intuition" also means

---

[1]See *The Power of Your Subconscious Mind* by Dr. Joseph Murphy, Prentice-Hall, Inc., Englewood Cliffs, N.J., 1963.

"inner hearing." Hearing is not the only way to nurture intuition. Sometimes it comes as a thought, but the most common way is to "hear the voice." Intuition goes much farther than reason. You employ reason to carry out intuition. Oftentimes you will find that intuition is the opposite of what your reasoning would have told you.

The conscious mind of man is reasoning, analytical and inquisitive; the subjective faculty of intuition is always spontaneous. It comes as a beacon to the conscious intellect. Many times it speaks as a warning against a proposed trip or plan of action. We must listen and learn to heed the voice of wisdom. It does not always speak to you when you wish it to do so, but only when you need it.

She Had a Persistent Feeling That
She Should Not Accept the Position

We will call her Louise Barrows (not her real name). She said to me: "I had this wonderful offer of a position, at twice my present salary, plus fringe benefits and the opportunity to travel to foreign lands, all expenses paid. It looks very good from every angle and my mother insists that I accept, but I can't, as I have a persistent feeling not to accept."

I suggested that she follow her intuitive feeling, which she did. Subsequently, she discovered that the organization had gone bankrupt and was involved in litigation with the government.

Her conscious mind was correct on the facts objectively known, but the nature of the organization, the motivation of the executives and ulterior plans of promotion were known to the intuitive faculties of Louise. Before she permitted her objective mind to argue with her inner knowledge, she came to a quick decision which proved to be correct in every way. She told me that she has made it a habit, after praying about anything, to follow the first impression, which she has found is always correct.

The Riches of Clairaudience

Clairaudience is a faculty of your subconscious mind and means "clear hearing." The daemon of Socrates is a classical case. He believed he could clearly hear the inner voice, whose admonitions were always wise. The voice was usually one of warning. Moreover, he pointed out that its strongest manifestations were made when his safety or well-being was involved. His subconscious mind communicated with the conscious mind in words audible to his senses.

This phenomenon is known as *clairaudience,* and it is based on the most powerful instinct of the human soul — the instinct of self-preservation. Socrates believed that the silence of the daemon was an approval of his conduct, and according to his belief was it done unto him.

How the Voice of Intuition Proved to Be a Life-Saver

A young woman, a member of our organization, was invited to visit some relatives in a distant city over Labor Day weekend. Her hosts said they would have another guest pick her up and take her along with her to Fresno. Immediately, while conversing with her cousin on the phone, the inner voice spoke clearly and said: "Stay home! Stay home!" She followed the advice and declined the invitation. The girl who was to pick her up was killed on the way.

For quite some time this young lady has directed her subconscious mind to supply her with guidance and knows that Divine right action will govern her. She has constantly affirmed that she will be instantaneously warned by the wisdom of her subconscious about anything she needs to know for her welfare and spiritual protection. It has never failed her. Through repetition she has conditioned her subconscious to respond, and the intelligence enables her conscious mind to receive communication from her subjective mind by means of spoken words. It is one way of bringing the wisdom of her deeper mind to her surface or objective mind. The sound she hears does not cause atmospheric vibrations.

These sounds or mental stimuli are distinct to her but are not perceptible to others who may be near her. You can employ this technique with fabulous dividends in all phases of your life.

A Banker Discovers the Riches of Intuition

A banker friend of mine, who specializes in gold stocks and investments for himself and special customers, has had extraordinary success in this field. Some months ago, the name of a foreign gold stock welled up in his mind, and his inner voice said, "Buy it." He did so and also advised many customers to do so. He also intuitively knew the price it would reach within a year. He and his bank customers have made profits of thousands of dollars.

He has been charging his subconscious mind as follows: "My subconscious mind will make me instantly aware of the right gold stock to purchase at the right time in the right way, which will bless me and my customers." Obviously, he has succeeded in getting the intuitive faculty of his subconscious to respond according to the nature of his request. The magic of extrasensory perception was alert to his request and presented him with the information at the right time.

A Most Extraordinary Experience

An ex-alcoholic once confessed to the author that at one time he had been in the throes of a deep depression due, as he said, to the poignant experience of the death of his wife and children in a car crash. He had placed a pistol to his head intending to commit suicide, when he immediately heard the commanding words in his ear, "Not, now, with long life will I satisfy you." He was stunned and desisted from his idea of suicide. That was forty years ago, and he is still vital, alert and alive and immensely successful in his profession.

It is well-known and understood that in all cases where danger to the individual is imminent, the subjective mind makes a supreme effort to avoid and prevent the danger. It acts and speaks in a way to which the individual will respond. The highest activity of your subconscious, or subjective mind (I use these words interchangeably), is exercised in the effort to preserve the life of man.

Remember, the monitions of your deeper self are always lifeward and should be heeded. That inner voice that seeks to protect you physically, financially and in all ways is not from supernatural agencies or disembodied entities but from the intuitive faculty of your own subconscious, which knows all and sees all.

A Remarkable Encounter in London, England

Last year I lectured in England. My sister informed me that there was a cousin of ours living in London, a man I had gone to school with many years ago. She had no idea where he lived or what his occupation was, but a friend of hers had told her he was living in London. His name was not in the telephone book.

I imagined myself meeting him, shaking hands with him and conversing about old times. I did this every night before I went to sleep in St. Ermin's Hotel. Only four hours remained of my week's stay in London before I was scheduled to leave for Switzerland. I went across the street to the post office around the corner to mail some letters and buy some English postage stamps. There, I heard a voice saying, "Well, Joe! Fancy meeting you here."

What I had pictured and felt as true in my mind had come true. The wisdom of my subconscious mind had brought both of us together in Divine order. The ways of the deeper levels of your mind are past finding out. Let the wonders and riches of intuition happen to you.

MEDITATION FOR THE RICHES OF THE SILENCE

"Jesus said, 'God is a Spirit; and they that worship him must worship him in spirit and in truth.'

"I know and realize that God is a spirit moving within me. I know that God is a feeling or deep conviction of harmony, health and peace within me; it is the movement of my own heart. The spirit or feeling of confidence and of faith which now possesses me is the spirit of God and the action of God on the waters of my mind; this is God; it is the creative Power within me.

"I live, move and have my being in the faith and confidence that goodness, truth and beauty shall follow me all the days of my life; this faith in God and all things good is omnipotent; it removes all barriers.

"I now close the door of the senses; I withdraw all attention from the world. I turn within to the One, the Beautiful, and the Good; here, I dwell with my Father beyond time and space; here, I live, move and dwell in the shadow of the Almighty. I am free from all fear, from the verdict of the world, and the appearance of things. I now feel His Presence, which is the feeling of the answered prayer, or the presence of my good.

"I become that which I contemplate. I now feel that I am what I want to be, this feeling or awareness is the action of God in me; it is the creative Power. I give thanks for the joy of the answered prayer and I rest in the silence that 'It is done.'"

CHAPTER POINTS TO REMEMBER

1. Your subconscious mind seeks to protect you at all times, and it behooves you to learn to listen to its inner monitions and promptings at all times.

2. When you are relaxed and your mind is at peace, the inner voice of intuition is heard clearly and distinctly.

3. The inner voice ofttimes speaks to you as an inner, persistent feeling, a sort of "hunch" warning you of danger to yourself or a loved one. A mother followed her "hunch" and was able to get prompt assistance for her son.

4. When you have a sincere desire for the truth, and knowing that Infinite Spirit responds according to the nature of your thought, you will get results. Affirm boldly that Infinite Intelligence is your constant guide and counselor and that you will instantly recognize the monitions of your Higher Self. You will receive answers according to your request.

5. You will receive answers and directions from your subconscious according to what you meditate on.

6. Artists, poets, inventors, etc. listen to the inner voice of intuition. They astonish the world by the beauties and glories drawn from the storehouse within.

7. A Japanese student of *The Power of Your Subconscious Mind*[2] heard an inner voice saying clearly to him, "Don't go on the plane." He followed the instruction. Shortly thereafter, that particular plane was involved in the greatest air disaster in Japan. He has trained his subconscious mind to watch over him in all his ways.

8. Intuition means direct perception of truths or facts independent of any reasoning process. Intuition also means, "inner hearing."

9. The extrasensory faculties of your deeper mind can see the motivations of an employer and also the future result. These are hidden from the conscious mind. When that intuitive feeling wells up telling you not to take the promotion, follow it.

10. After praying about anything specific, the first impression is usually correct.

11. Clairaudience is a faculty of your subconscious and means "clear hearing." Self-preservation is the most powerful instinct of the human soul, and many

---

[2]See *The Power of Your Subconscious Mind* by Dr. Joseph Murphy, Prentice-Hall, Inc., Englewood Cliffs, N.J., 1963.

times your subjective self speaks in a voice to warn you and to protect you.

12. You can direct your subconscious to guide you always and know that Divine right action governs you and that you are to be instantly informed about anything you need to know for your protection. You may hear a voice saying, "Don't go" — obey it.

13. A banker conveys the idea to his subconscious mind that he will be instantly made aware of the right gold stock to purchase, and the names of particular gold stocks well up from his subconscious, and he becomes consciously aware of the right gold stock to buy.

14. In all cases where danger to the individual is imminent, the subjective mind makes a supreme effort to avoid danger. It may speak in a way to which the individual will respond.

15. The monitions of your deeper mind are always lifeward and should be heeded.

16. If you wish to meet someone and you don't know where the person is, picture yourself talking to the individual, feel the reality of the experience, dramatize it in your mind and enter into the tones of reality. Your deeper mind will bring both of you together in Divine order.

17. How to avail yourself of the amazing riches of the silence is contained in the meditation at the end of the chapter.

thirteen

How Your Money Dreams
Can Make You Rich —
The Secret of Psychic Osmosis

Emerson, in his essay on self-reliance, says: "Trust thyself: Every heart vibrates to that iron string. Accept the place the Divine Providence has found for you, the society of your contemporaries, the connection of events. Great men have always done so and confided themselves child-like to the genius of their age, betraying their perception that the absolute trustworthy was seated at their heart, working through their hands, predominating in all their being."

Here Emerson is telling every man that God indwells him, that the absolute trustworthy was seated in his heart and that all man has to do is to permit himself to vibrate or tune in on the Infinite within and receive all the blessings and riches of life. Moreover, Emerson is saying that you are Life, or God manifested, and that you are an instrument of Life's expression. You are unique; there is no one in all the world like you, because you are you. Your thumbprint and toeprint are different and the rhythm of your heart and the secretions of your glands are different from those of any other person. Infinite differentiation is the law of life. Your thoughts, your attitude toward life, and your belief and convictions undoubtedly are different from others.

You were born with certain endowments, talents, abilities and special inherent gifts. You are here to express more and more of the God-Presence and to experience the joy of living the life more abundant. You are uniquely equipped to express life in a way and manner that no one else in all the world can do. You want to be what you want to be, you want to do what you love to do, and you want to have all the good things of life.

You can achieve all these goals in life because you are endowed with the qualities and faculties of imagination, thought, reason and the power to choose and act. Let Life flow through you as harmony, beauty, love, joy, health, wealth and fullness of expression.

How a Teacher Instills the Riches of Self-Confidence in His Boys

Is it not written in your law, I said, Ye are gods? (John 10:34).

A young man who teaches Sunday School in Las Vegas told me that he had quite a number of young boys who were shy, timid, and diffident and who generally had a profound inferiority complex. He said that he wrote down on the blackboard for each one to copy and affirm for five minutes prior to sleep every night the following:

"I am a son of the Living God. God loves me and cares for me. I am different, and God wants to do something special through me. God watches over me and guides me, as I am growing in strength, love and wisdom. My Heavenly Father loves his son. He walks and talks in me."

He had each boy write the above affirmation down and then instructed them that as they used it and affirmed it every day, there would be a response from the God-Presence and that they would grow in wisdom, strength and power and would become outstanding students, successful in college, and wealthy and rich in all the blessings of life. He said that it did his heart good to see these boys expand, blossom and grow in confidence and self-reliance. All of this was reflected in their relationships to their fathers and mothers and in their work at school. They seemed to flower in a most wonderful way. Ten of the very shy boys who had felt very inferior have graduated from high school, obtained scholarships, and have advanced and progressed beyond the teacher's fondest dreams.

Actually, all he did was to instill into the minds and hearts of these boys the knowledge that God indwells them and that He would respond to the simple prayer of their hearts and help them to become famous and outstanding. They realized, as Emerson said, that the absolutely trustworthy was seated at their heart working through them at all times.

The True Meaning of Self-Confidence

Confidence means "with faith." Faith is a way of thinking, an attitude of mind, an understanding of the laws of mind. It is an awareness that your thought and feeling create your destiny. You have faith when you know that any idea felt as true by your conscious mind will be impressed on and accepted by your subconscious mind and come to pass on the screen of space. In simple, everyday language, your faith is an awareness of the presence and power of God (the Living Spirit Almighty) within you. Through your contact with this Presence and through the medium of your thought you can live a victorious and triumphant life. You will find yourself meeting all obstacles, difficulties and challenges head on, realizing that they are all Divinely outmatched. Tuning in on the Divine Presence within you, you can move through the vicissitudes of life with a deep abiding trust that you can do all things through the God-Power which strengthens you.

How He Developed Self-Confidence
and Became Rich and Successful

Recently a businessman who had failed three times in business came to see me. He was down on himself, felt inferior and full of self-criticism. I explained to him that he should be full of faith and confidence because within him is Infinite Intelligence, which created the world and knows no obstacles, and which can reveal to him everything he needs to know. He was born to succeed and triumph in life, because Infinite Intelligence, or God, cannot fail. There is nothing to oppose, challenge or vitiate the movement of Omnipotence.

Accordingly, I gave him a specific formula for success and riches, while explaining to him that confidence in the God-Self within him is contagious, causing him to radiate assurance, faith, poise and balance, so that he becomes a spiritual and mental magnet, attracting good to himself from all sides.

One of the most important of all the spiritual gems of truth in the Bible is found in Romans: *If God be for us, who can be against us?* (Romans 8:31).

Here is the specific formula that simply worked wonders for this businessman. Every morning after shaving, brushing his teeth and combing his hair, he looked directly into the mirror and said aloud feelingly and knowingly: "If God be for me, who can be against me? I can do all things through the God-Power which strengthens me. Success is mine and riches are mine. Thank you, Father."

He repeated these great Biblical truths for four or five minutes every morning, knowing that as he was sincere, these truths would penetrate by osmosis from his conscious mind to his subconscious; and since the law of his subconscious is compulsive, he would be compelled to express success and riches.

A few weeks passed, he met a widow, married her, and they are extremely happy. She placed a quarter of a million dollars at his disposal, enabling him to open a new business. With his wife as secretary and treasurer of the new corporation, they are going ahead financially by leaps and bounds.

Such experiences are commonplace today with men and women who begin to tap the tremendous potentials within them. I read recently that there were more millionaires now in the United States than at any time in history.

Allow Yourself Success and the Riches of the Infinite

The Life-Principle, which some call God, is forever seeking to express Itself at higher levels through you. There is an inner urge in you always prompting you in the form of a desire to rise higher and higher. This Presence and Power is all-wise, knows all and sees all, and is omnipotent and supreme. Insist on the best in life; refuse the second best. Concentrate your thought, feeling and attention on your profession, realizing that the infinite intelligence of your subconscious is constantly revealing to you new creative ideas and better ways in which to serve.

Realize that you are one with the Infinite and that the Infinite cannot fail. Emerson says: "No one can cheat you out of ultimate success but yourself." Carlyle said: "The wealth of a man is the number of things he loves and blesses which he is loved and blessed by." Coleridge wrote:

> He prayeth well who loveth well
> Both man and bird and beast.
> He prayeth best who loveth best
> All things both great and small;
> For the dear God who loveth us,
> He made and loveth all.

It is not fate that blocks your success or riches, nor lack of money, introductions or contacts. It is yourself. All you have to do is to change your thought-life and keep it changed. Let your habitual thinking be: "Success is mine, God's wealth is mine, harmony is mine, and I am a channel for all the riches of God." Your thoughts are creative and you become what you think all day long.

The Riches of a Practical and Working Faith

Millions of people have faith in creeds, dogmas, sects, traditions, amulets, charms, icons, shrines, etc., but they have no real workable faith at all, and their lives are chaotic and confused. Millions suffer from lack and poor health and barely eke out a living because they are unaware of how to tap the treasure of infinity in their own subconscious mind.

Millions of other people have a real workable faith which they demonstrate in their bodies, their business, their finances, their human relations and in all other phases of their lives. Man's faith in God must be personally demonstrated and it will appear in the light in his eyes; his affluence, demonstrating his faith in the law of opulence, will surely be indicative, as will his trust and understanding of the bountiful nature of the providence of God. Man reflects his confidence in himself and the powers within him by his positive manner, gestures, speech and the sunshine of his smile.

A Widow Discovers the Riches of Self-Confidence

A widow with two sons consulted me with the usual complaint: "It's hard for me to make ends meet. I'm lonesome. My boys don't have the right clothes and the right food. I get $120 a week take-home pay," etc.

I gave her a simple technique, as well as an explanation, as follows. Conceive of yourself now as successful. In your mind's eye, visualize a lovely home with a den for the boys. See them playing there. Feel beautiful clothes on you, including a sable coat or a mink, whichever you prefer. Touch the coat in your imagination, feel a beautiful diamond on your finger, and hear me pronouncing the words, "I now pronounce you man and wife." Hear your regular bank clerk congratulating you on your big deposit.

I said to her, "Remain faithful to this picture in your mind. You want to be married, and feeling the ring on your finger means to you that you are in the process of being married to the ideal, spiritual-minded man, and hearing the words, 'I now pronounce you man and wife' means it has already happened in your mind, and what has happened in your mind must take place objectively, irrespective of any seeming difficulties and obstacles that seem to stand between you and the realization of your mental image. You will triumph, become wealthy, and you will also be happy, joyous and free."

Quietly, this widow began to think of riches for herself and her sons. She also began to feel how happy, joyous and thrilled she would be if she met some man who was spiritually oriented, congenial and harmonious. In this mood, she began to thank the God-Presence within her for riches, success and companionship prior to sleep. She did this each night for about a week. At the end of about ten days, she met a bachelor who was introduced to her by a mutual friend. He proved to be the perfect answer to all her dreams and meditations.

Realize there is always an answer. There is "Someone who cares" — that One Who created you loves you and watches over you at all times, asleep or awake.

A Salesman Discovers the Riches of Self-Confidence

A young man who was selling land said to me, "The economic conditions are bad," "Times are slow," "Business is bad." He was giving attention to lack and limitation. Naturally, he experienced a lack of sales. He had a sense of inadequacy and timidity.

I suggested to him that if he made it a point to suggest constructive statements many times a day to his subconscious, everything would change. My secretary typed out a card for him with the following statements, which he was instructed to use twelve or thirteen times a day: "I have perfect faith in God's supply and in God's guidance. I know that all who buy land are prospered and blessed. Infinite Intelligence attracts buyers to me who have the money, who want the land and who rejoice in its possession. I am blessed and they are blessed. I am strong in the Lord and in the power of His might. Divine activity and immediate, perfect results now take place in my life, and I give thanks for the miracles in my life."

By carrying this card with him and repeating these truths frequently, he restored his confidence in his sales ability, and he began to sell, prosper and expand along all lines. He said to me at the Wilshire Ebell Theatre where I give public lectures, "Miracles are happening in my life. I sold land to the value of a half a million dollars this week in the Valley."

God's blessings never cease. Open your mind and heart and receive all the wealth you could want for yourself.

MEDITATION FOR THE RICHES OF FAITH

"Jesus said, 'Thy faith hath made thee whole.'

"I positively believe in the Healing Power of God within me. My conscious and subconscious mind are in perfect agreement. I accept the statement of truth which I positively affirm. The words I speak are words of spirit and they are truth.

"I now decree that the Healing Power of God is transforming my whole body, making me whole, pure, and perfect. I believe with a deep, inner certitude that my prayer of faith is being manifested now. I am guided by the Wisdom of God in all matters. The Love of God flows in transcendent beauty and loveliness into my mind and body, transforming, restoring and energizing every atom of my being. I sense the peace that passeth understanding. God's Glory surrounds me, and I rest forever in the Everlasting Arms."

CHAPTER POINTS TO REMEMBER

1. Emerson says to trust thyself: "Every heart vibrates to that iron string." Join up with God within you,

realizing that all things are possible to God. Place absolute trust in this Presence to respond to your call and aid you in the fulfillment of your dreams.

2. You are unique. There is no one in all the world like you. You are endowed with certain qualities, abilities and capacities. As you claim, "God reveals my true expression," doors will open up and you will be Divinely expressed and in your true place in life, doing what you love to do, Divinely happy and Divinely prospered.

3. If you are teaching a group of boys in Sunday School, teach them that they are sons of God and that God loves them and cares for them. Have them affirm these truths frequently, knowing that there will be an immediate response from the God-Presence within them and that God will reveal his wonders in a different way through each boy. As you do this, they will grow in self-confidence and self-reliance.

4. Confidence means "with faith." Have faith that when you call on Infinite Intelligence It responds to you. You build up your faith when you realize that thoughts are creative; what you feel you attract, and what you imagine you become. Any idea felt as true will be impressed on your subconscious mind and come to pass. This knowledge gives you faith in the laws of your mind and its practice will work wonders in your life.

5. A magic formula for building self-confidence and success is to look in the mirror in the morning and then for about five minutes to affirm: "If God be for me, who can be against me? I can do all things through the God-Power which strengthens me." Make a habit of this and you will be full of self-confidence and faith in all things good, and wonders will happen in your life.

6. Insist on the best in life and the best will come into your life. "No one can cheat you out of ultimate success but yourself" — Emerson. Realize you are one with the Infinite and the Infinite cannot fail.

7. You must have a workable faith. In other words, you must demonstrate your faith in God and all things good. It must appear in your home, in your relationships with people, in your finances, and in your net worth. Faith without demonstration and results is dead. Have faith in the creative laws of your mind which never fail and never change.

8. Conceive of yourself now as successful and wealthy. Imagine the reality of the state, and irrespective of seeming obstacles and difficulties, you will experience the result of your mental image. Your mental image is absolute monarch and king, and as you give it your attention, faith and confidence, it must come to pass.

9. There is always an answer. There is Someone who cares — that One Who created you and the universe. Trust It. It is the One, the Beautiful and the Good.

10. When selling land, realize what you are seeking is also seeking you. Claim boldly that Infinite Intelligence attracts to you buyers who have the money and want the land, and who will prosper with it and be happy. They are blessed and you are blessed. Claim Divine activity and realize that since God's blessings and God's riches never cease flowing into your experience, miracles will happen in your life. The day will break for you and all the shadows will flee away.

11. Repeat the meditation at the end of the chapter for the never-failing Riches of Faith.

fourteen

How to Use the Amazing Law That Reveals All Money Secrets

Love is always outgoing. It is an emanation. Love must have an object. You can fall in love with music, art, a great project, an enterprise, science, and many other things. You can always fall deeply in love with the great principles and eternal verities which never change. Love is an emotional attachment to your ideal, your cause, your scheme or your profession.

Einstein loved the principles of mathematics and they revealed their secrets to him. That is what loves does. You can fall in love with astronomy and it will reveal to you its secrets. How much do you want what you want? Do you want to leave your old ideas, the traditional view of things and get new ideas, new imagery and new viewpoints? Are you open and receptive? Do you want good digestion? If you do, you must give up resentment, and your pet peeves and grudges. Do you want wealth and success? If so, you must be willing to accept the riches within and without.

Realize that you are born to succeed, for the Infinite within you can't fail. You have to leave your jealousies, envies and any of the false concepts you may have of God and enter into the joy of abundant and richer living.

How an Actor Proved the Riches of Love

An actor said to me, "I fear I am going to fail. I am going to crack up on the stage. I am going to say the wrong thing." His vivid imagination was on failure. I explained to him that he was the master, a king in charge of his thoughts, ideas, imagery and responses; that he was the absolute monarch issuing the orders to his mind and body, which automatically obeyed him; that he had the authority to order his thoughts around and to instruct them to give attention to his ideal and the power of God within him. Furthermore, I advised that all he had to do was to fall in love with a new concept, a new estimate, a new blueprint of himself.

He Practiced the Following Victory Formula

He affirmed frequently: "From now on, I give all my allegiance, devotion and loyalty to the God-Self within which is none other than my Higher Self. I know that love of my Higher Self means to have a healthy, reverent, wholesome respect for the Divinity within me which is all powerful and all wise. From now on, I know that love of God is to refuse to give power to any person, place or thing, but to give my supreme allegiance to the One Presence and Power within me. I know I can do all things through the God-Power which strengthens me. I now imagine I am playing a role before a distinguished audience. I live the role; I feel entranced, fascinated and absorbed in the drama; and I hear loved ones congratulating me. It is wonderful."

This actor began to affirm these truths three or four times a day. Also, he played a vivid, imaginary scene, and he fell in love with a nobler, grander concept of himself. All fear vanished because love casts out fear. The love he exuded was his emotional attachment to his ideal of a magnificent performance. Today he commands a fabulous income, all because he began to exalt God in the midst of him.

There is no fear in love. Perfect love casteth out fear (I John 4:18).

The Riches of Love Saved His Life

Recently a young officer who returned from Vietnam told me that on one of his night patrols he and his men were ambushed. Bullets were striking all around him, and suddenly he found himself all alone. He said that all he could remember were a few passages from the Psalms and that he seemed to be frozen to the ground. He repeated: *Under his wings shalt thou trust* (Psalm 91:4). *The Lord is my light and my salvation* (Psalm 27:1). *The Lord is the strength of my life; of whom shall I be afraid?* (Psalm 27:1).

As he repeated these truths, an inner sense of peace came over him, and he felt a deep sense of security; he was Divinely led to safety and was picked up by a helicopter the next morning. All of his men were killed in that ambush. He said to me, "I talked to Him and He responded."

He Discovered the Riches of the Law of Love

Recently a doctor told me about a patient of his, an old friend, who had run up a bill of over $3,000 and was very slow in paying. He had been very lenient with her, but he knew she had inherited $100,000, and so he asked her for payment. She became very bitter and sarcastic, and accused him of giving her the wrong vitamins. She said his treatments were no good, etc. He said that he let her explode and walked away.

He said to himself that rather than turn the bill over to a collection agency, he would put into application the law of love. Accordingly, in his morning and evening meditation, he affirmed that Mrs. Jones (not her real name) was honest, loving, kind, and at peace, and that God's love and harmony saturated her whole being. He imagined that she was right in front of him, saying, "Here is the check; I am grateful. God bless you."

He did this for a few minutes night and morning, and at the end of a few days, the result was astonishing. This wealthy woman came to visit him and expressed profound apologies while tendering to him payment of $5,000, not $3,000, which she owed. He had discovered the riches of the law of love. You will notice that he did not retaliate or criticize her in any way. He simply surrounded her with God's love and peace, and Divine right action took place.

The Riches of Love Never Fail

Love is an outreaching of the heart. It is goodwill to all. If you are working in an office, factory or store, it pays you fabulous dividends to wish for all those around you health, happiness, peace, promotion, wealth and all the blessings of life. As you radiate love and goodwill to all, and as you wish riches and promotion for them, you will at the same time bless and prosper yourself. Remember, what you wish for another, you wish for yourself, and what you withhold from another, you are withholding from yourself.

You are the only thinker in your universe, and your thoughts are creative; therefore, it is plain, common sense to have goodwill for others and to radiate love and all the blessings of life to them. A president of a big chain told me a few days ago that the reason for ninety per cent of the dismissals from his organization is not because of incompetence, stealing or tardiness, but the inability of individuals to get along with their co-workers and customers.

Love is the fulfilling of the law (Romans 13:10). The love spoken of in the Bible is not a sentiment or a Hollywood confection. Love is the cohesive force that unites families and nations, and which keeps the whole world and the galaxies in space moving rhythmically, harmoniously and peacefully through eons of time. Love is the law of health, happiness, peace, prosperity and joyous and successful living. The children of love are harmony, health, peace, kindness, joy, honesty, integrity, justice and laughter.

Begin now to radiate all the blessings of life to all those around you and to all people everywhere. Salute the Divinity in the other and silently realize for him or her: "The riches of God are flowing through you." You will be amazed at how you prosper. Showers of blessings will be yours.

The Infinite Riches of Love's Healing Balm

The late Dr. Harry Gaze, who was a famous international lecturer on mental and spiritual laws, told of a man in London who was wasting away due to tuberculosis. This man's spiritual advisor discovered that he hated bankers, brokers and all wealthy people, this feeling stemming from early childhood when he had witnessed his father being dispossessed of their home because he defaulted in payment to the local banker; so the boy generalized from the particular and hated all bankers and rich people.

His spiritual advisor told him to go down to the London Stock Exchange and stand for one hour on the street near the building, and for every single person, man or woman, who passed by, he was to affirm: "God's love fills your soul. The riches of God are yours now." The man did as he was told, albeit reluctantly at first, but he kept his bargain, and as he consciously and deliberately expressed love and riches to all, it came back multiplied, pressed down, shaken together and running over.

Dr. Gaze said this man had experienced a remarkable healing. Sputum tests and all other types of examinations by Harley Street specialists showed he was completely healed. This man got a job in a prominent banking firm and became very successful as well as immensely wealthy. Divine love became alive in his heart, in his body, and also in his pocketbook.

The Riches in Loving Your Wife, Husband and Children in the Right Way

Claim that he or she is alive with the love of God and that His love saturates and permeates his or her whole being. Picture your loved one in your mind's eye surrounded by the light of God's love. Realize that this healing light of God's love enfolds, enwraps, encompasses and illumines his or her mind, and body. Wonders happen as you pray this way.

She Found the Healing Power of Love

A young secretary who had been using various lotions to keep her face free from skin eruptions that she termed acne, found that they nevertheless persisted. At my suggestion, she gave herself the mirror treatment following the injunction of the Bible: *His flesh shall be fresher than a child's: he shall return to the days of his youth* (Job 33:25).

We changed the verse somewhat, and as she looked in the mirror every morning, she affirmed: "My skin is an envelope of God's love. It is without spot and blemish. It is fresher than a child's, and the radiance of youth and beauty saturate my whole being."

Her face cleared up in a few weeks, and it is now as soft and beautiful as she desired, radiating the sunshine of God's love.

The Riches of Love Bring Justice in a Lawsuit

During a talk with a woman who was terribly frustrated by a prolonged lawsuit lasting over five years, she pointed out how unfair the judge had been in the first instance and stated that it is now going to the Court of Appeals. She said one witness deliberately lied and swore falsely, adding that it was all so unfair.

I suggested she pray night and morning as follows: "All those involved in this court case are surrounded by the sacred circle of God's love. God's love, truth and harmony reign supreme in the minds and hearts of all involved. They are all known in Divine Mind, and the law of love prevails." This prayer dissolved all bitterness, resentment and hostility lodged in her subconscious mind.

Her opponent in the lawsuit died on the way to court one morning, and his family settled the matter out of court and actually were delighted to do so. She was perfectly satisfied with the settlement.

The Riches of the Protecting Power of Love

A doctor friend of mine told me that one of his psychotic patients had put a gun to his head and said, "God told me to kill you." The doctor said calmly, "God changed His mind, because he told me this morning what to do to heal you and make you a great, illumined soul." The doctor said, "God indwells you and God indwells me. God can't contradict Himself. God is love, and He wants you whole and perfect now."

The psychotic gave him the gun and he had the man placed in a mental institution for treatment. The doctor is a spiritual-minded man, and he knew that his contemplation of God's Presence in the patient would be felt by him. *Perfect love casteth out fear* (I John 4:18).

Love Unites and Love Heals

Your wife, your husband, your son and your daughter need to feel loved, wanted, appreciated and important in the scheme of things. A man said to me recently, "The reason I have a mistress is because she makes me feel so important. She praises my accomplishments and tells me how wonderful I am, how brilliant I am, what a marvelous conversationalist I am and how clever and brilliant I am in my profession. She makes me feel like a king."

I asked him, "What about your wife? She bore you four children. She is loyal, devoted, sincere and a marvelous mother."

"That's true," he said, "but I'm nobody when I go home. I get no recognition. She nags me."

I explained to him that many women nag because they get no appreciation, attention and praise. Moreover, a wife subconsciously detects your infidelity. He did not want a divorce, and I brought both of them together. They decided that love was really there but dormant and never openly expressed. For many years neither one of them had expressed their love for one another. They took each other for granted.

To preserve the marriage, both began a prayer process, he with the 91st Psalm every night and she with the 27th Psalm every morning. Both agreed to radiate love, peace and harmony to each other regularly and systematically. Each agreed to affirm for the other five minutes every day: "God's love fills your soul. I love you."

Love united them again in a Divine embrace, for love is the universal solvent. Only God and His love can and does heal the wounds of mankind.

MEDITATION: LOVE AND GOODWILL PROSPER ME

"'All ye are brethren, for one is your father.' I always bring harmony, peace and joy into every situation and into all of my personal relationships. I know, believe and claim that the peace of God reigns supreme in the mind and heart of everyone in my home and business. No matter what the problem is, I always maintain peace, poise, patience and wisdom. I fully and freely forgive everyone, regardless of what they may have said or done. I cast all my burdens on the God-self within; I go free; this is a marvelous feeling. I know that blessings come to me as I forgive.

"I see the angel of God's Presence behind every problem or difficult situation. I know the solution is there and that everything is working out in Divine order. I trust the God-Presence implicitly; It has the know-how of accomplishment. The Absolute Order of Heaven and His Absolute Wisdom are acting through me now and at all times; I know that order is Heaven's first law.

"My mind is now fixed joyously and expectantly on this perfect harmony. I know the result is the inevitable, perfect solution; my answer is God's answer; it is Divine; for it is the melody of God's broadcast."

CHAPTER POINTS TO REMEMBER

1. Love is always outgoing. Love frees; it gives; it is the spirit of God in action. Love must have an object. You can fall in love with music, art, science, mathematics, or the truths of God. You can also fall in love with your Higher Self by recognizing It as the Source of all blessings. It is God in you.

2. You are the king and absolute monarch over your thoughts, images, ideas and responses. You can order your thoughts around like an employer instructing employees what to do. You can steer your thoughts correctly in the same way you steer your car.

3. Love of your Higher Self, or God, means you have a healthy, reverent, wholesome respect for the Divinity within you, which is all-powerful, all-wise, knows all and sees all. In other words, it means you give supreme allegiance to the Spirit within you, which is God; and that you absolutely refuse to give power to any created thing.

4. You can fall in love with a grander, greater, nobler concept of yourself by imagining you are doing what you love to do. Become absorbed and engrossed in the mental movie, and you will achieve your goal. Love of your ideal casts out all fear.

5. In the midst of an emergency, affirm: "The Lord is my light and my salvation; whom shall I fear? The Lord is the strength of my life; of whom shall I be afraid?" There will be a response and security will be yours.

6. When a person is abusive and refuses to pay a just debt, surround that person with light and love; feel and know that the love of God flows through the person and that the law of harmony prevails. A harmonious solution follows.

7. Radiate love, peace and goodwill to all people around you and to all people everywhere. Wish for them health, happiness, peace, abundance and all the blessings of life. As you make a habit of this, countless blessings will be yours. Ninety per cent of people who are failures in life don't get ahead because they rub others the wrong way. Love and goodwill is the answer.

8. Love is the fulfilling of the law of health, happiness, wealth and success. Love is goodwill to all, and what you wish for another you wish for yourself.

9. If resentful of others' wealth and success, affirm for everyone you see and meet: "God's love fills your soul and the riches of God are yours now." Wonders will happen in your life and you will be healed of jealousy and ill will, and you will prosper.

10. If married, tell your wife or husband, "I love you. God loves you." Feel it; believe it; proclaim it. Love unites and preserves the marriage.

11. If you have skin trouble, affirm: "My skin is an envelope of God's love and is without spot and blemish." Realize that Divine love dissolves everything unlike itself, and your skin will become whole, radiant and perfect.

12. If involved in a protracted and complicated lawsuit of any kind, realize that God's love flows through the minds and hearts of all involved and that there is a Divine solution through the harmony and love of God. See the happy ending and contemplate the Divine solution through the action of God's love, and victory and right action will be yours.

13. You can protect yourself by realizing God's love in the other and God's love saturating and surround-

ing you. Realize it is God talking to God, and you
will be protected and set free.

14. A married man who has a mistress usually claims
    that the reason is that she praises him and makes
    him feel outstanding and important. She stresses all
    his fine and good qualities. To preserve the mar-
    riage, see God in each other and exalt God in one
    another, and the marriage will grow more blessed
    through the years. Love unites. Love heals. Love
    restores the soul. God is love.

15. Using the meditation at the end of the chapter will
    prove most beneficial to you for all kinds of riches
    in daily living.

fifteen

How to Charge Yourself with Money-Magnetism

Ralph Waldo Emerson said, "Nothing can bring you peace but the triumph of principles." When you learn the way your mind works and direct it wisely, you will add to your peace, prosperity, poise, balance and security.

The engineer follows the principles of mathematics in building a bridge; he gains knowledge of stresses, strains and other complex scientific calculations based on immutable laws which are the same yesterday, today and forever.

The laws of your mind are referred to you again and again in the Bible, which says: *As thou hast believed, so be it done unto thee* (Matthew 8:13).

Excess tension interferes with the productive lives of thousands of people, bringing about frustration and many nervous disorders in its train. A certain amount of anxiety is normal and necessary. For example, the singer about to go on the stage is somewhat tense, which is an accumulation of energy and power which charges his mental and spiritual batteries, enabling him to overcome any sense of failure. It is excessive and prolonged tension which is dangerous. When the singer begins to sing, he ticks off that surplus energy in the same manner as a clock that is wound up ticks off the time. If you wind the clock too tightly, you break the spring, and then we have no song or time, either.

When you charge yourself with the feeling that you can do all things through the God-Power which strengthens you, you will give a wonderful performance.

How a Businessman Overcame
Tension and Anxiety Over His Debts

In talking to a businessman recently whom I met on the plane to Las Vegas, Nevada, he told me that about five years ago he had been deeply in debt, and that many of the wholesalers were pressing him for payment and threatening legal action. He said, "One night I sat down and read the 23rd Psalm, and then an idea welled up within me to make a list of all those to whom I owed money and the amounts. I wrote down each name with the exact amount following it, and then in my imagination I visited each one, giving him a check covering the exact amount owed. In my mind's eye, I saw each one smile and thank me, and also congratulate me. I felt the handshake of each one, saw the happy look on each face and heard each one say to me that my credit is good any time."

He said he repeated this mental imagery or movie scene over and over every night with sensory vividness, feeling the naturalness and joy of it all. Following the above prayer process, he felt a great sense of peace and tranquility, and at the end of about two weeks he had a very vivid and prophetic dream. A man appeared to him in this dream, instructing him to go to a certain casino and play certain numbers on the roulette, and he saw the amount he would win.

The following evening, he did exactly as he had been instructed to do in the dream and won $30,000 which paid off all his debts. He has not gambled since and realizes that the wisdom of his subconscious responded in its own unique way to his request. He looked at the happy ending in his meditation every night, and having seen and felt the joyous fulfillment of his prayer, he experienced the joy of the answered prayer. Money is really a thought-image in your mind. Your thoughts are things. Wealth is a state of mind, nothing more or less.

How to Banish Anxiety Over Debts

I have given the following prayer to many people over the years who have been burdened with debts and with unpaid bills piling up on them: "God is the Source of my supply. I know when I am anxious I do not trust God. The money I now possess is magnified and multiplied a thousand-fold. I realize all the money I have is a symbol of the infinite riches of God. I turn to the Infinite Presence within, knowing in my heart and soul It opens the way for me to pay all my debts, leaving me a vast surplus. I surrender a list of all these debts in the hands of my Heavenly Father, and I give thanks they are all paid in Divine order. God's riches are circulating in my life, and I rejoice and am exceedingly glad that every creditor is paid now, and God prospers me beyond my fondest dreams. I believe that I have received now, and I know that according to my faith is it done unto me. I know God will rain blessings from Heaven for me now."

I instruct each one in debt to claim these truths joyously, lovingly and with the understanding that there is always a response in accordance with his request. When anxious thoughts come to mind, he is never to think of bills or lack or debts, but smilingly give thanks for God's abundance and riches, and rejoice that the obligation is paid now. When this technique is followed faithfully, there is a reconditioning of the mind to wealth, and I have seen marvelous results follow. You can apply this prayer process and let wonders happen in your life.

Learn to Relax and Let Go and
Experience Riches All Around You

It is not hard to believe in the Invisible Source of supply. Your five senses reveal to you the world around you on this three-dimensional plane. Your ears are attuned to hear only a few octaves of sound, yet your radio and television reveal to you that all about you are symphonies, music, laughter, songs, drama, speeches and voices from thousands of miles away.

Your eyes are geared to see the physical objects around you, but the atmosphere is full of pictures of bullfights in Spain, ships at sea, operas, Cabinet meetings and the President presiding at news conferences. You do not see gamma rays, beta rays, alpha waves, radio waves and cosmic rays, yet the atmosphere is nevertheless teeming with these vibrations.

Your thought-image of wealth, money or sale of property which you don't see is first cause relative to that idea, and by accepting this truth and feeling the reality of it, your invisible thought-image will become money, riches or a home you need. Thoughts are things.

How a Secretary Overcame Anxiety
and Tension in the Office

A legal secretary complained to me that there was a lot of strife and contention in her office. She added that there was considerable intrigue and undermining among the staff and employees. The remedy I suggested was to explain to her that no one could really disturb her but herself. She disturbed herself by her own thoughts, by her reaction to what was happening. If you stop and think, you will observe that it is always the movement of your own thought that disturbs you.

The suggestions, statements and actions of others have no power to disturb or annoy you unless you transfer the power in yourself to them and say to yourself, "He or she has power to irritate me." Then you are enthroning false gods in your mind. Your harmony, peace, health or wealth is not dependent on others. Enthrone God in your mind. Let God be your employer, boss, paymaster, adjuster and troubleshooter.

I suggested to this secretary that she use the following spiritual formula regularly: "God's love governs me at work. I have no opinion about others. I judge not; therefore, I cannot suffer or be disturbed. The peace and harmony of God govern me and all that I do. Every anxious thought is completely stilled, for I am working for God, and His peace fills my soul. The confidence and joy of God enfold me at all times. All who work in the office are God's sons and daughters, and each one contributes to the peace, harmony, prosperity and success of this office. Divine love comes in the door of our office; and Divine love governs the minds and hearts of all in the office; and Divine love goes out the door. God is my boss, my paymaster, my guide and my counsellor, and I recognize no other. I give all power and recognition to God and I walk serenely and peacefully in His light. I laugh, I sing and I rejoice. God works wonders in my life."

She repeated this prayer every morning before going to work and every night prior to sleep and quickly built up an immunity to all negative suggestions and thoughts of those around her. When someone was obnoxious, surly or sarcastic, she would silently say to herself, "I salute the Divinity in you. God thinks, speaks and acts through you." Nothing bothered her, nothing moved her, nothing disturbed her and nothing frightened her. She had found God within herself and that was sufficient.

I had the joy of conducting the marriage ceremony for this young lady, who married the president of the corporation she worked for. He said to me, "She is the most radiant and angelic of all the girls in our office." Knowing how to pray paid her fabulous dividends. It will do the same for you.

How a Student Overcame His Anxiety
That He Would Fail His Examinations

A college student in his final year said to me, "I'm all tensed up, full of anxiety. I study in my room at night but it all goes out of my mind the next day and I have failed in some examinations. I freeze up. I read the Old Testament every night, but it does not help."

I explained to him that his trouble was the continuous feeling of anxiety and tension; that he goes to class afraid he can't remember and to the examination afraid he will fail. In that state of stress, the mind establishes a block and the answers which are in the subconscious mind will not come to the surface mind. I said to him, "You read the Old Testament but you don't practice it, eh?"

I gave this young man a spiritual formula, suggesting that every night, before beginning to study, he pray and affirm the following: *Acquaint now thyself with him, and be at peace: thereby good shall come unto thee* (Job 22:21). *When he giveth quietness, who then can make trouble?* (Job 34:29). *For thus saith the Lord God, the Holy One of Israel; In returning and rest shall ye be saved; in quietness and in confidence shall be your strength* (Isaiah 30:15). *For God is not the author of confusion, but of peace* (I Corinthians 14:33). *Great peace have they which love thy law; and nothing shall offend them* (Psalm 119:165).

He saturated his mind every night with these great truths, absorbing and mentally digesting them. He imagined these truths sinking into his subconscious mind like seeds deposited in the soil, and becoming a part of him. He made a mental adjustment and focussed his attention on God's river of peace and power, and no longer fixed his attention on his problems.

His mind was now stayed on God, and just prior to sleep every night, he affirmed: "I have a perfect memory for everything I need to know, and I˜pass all examinations in Divine order, and I give thanks." He is on top of his problem and is relaxed mentally, spiritually and physically. His anxieties have been lifted and his talent and memory were set free. As he saturated his mind with these age-old Biblical truths, he neutralized all the negative patterns in his subconscious mind and became transformed by the renewal of his mind.

How an Executive Overcame Anxiety Over His Business Situation

Recently I interviewed a businessman who said to me that his doctor had diagnosed his case as "anxiety neurosis." He added that he was terribly tense, suffered from insomnia, and was anxious about money, the future, his children and inflation.

I explained to him that a certain amount of tension is good. For example, steel without tension would not be considered good steel. I added that what his doctor meant is undoubtedly abnormally misdirected tension or energy. I suggested that he cooperate with his doctor, but I also told him to practice the great therapy of words.

The way he overcame his anxiety neurosis was as follows. He began to have quiet sessions with himself three or four times a day, at which times he affirmed quietly and lovingly: "My feet are relaxed, my ankles are relaxed, the calves of my legs are relaxed, my abdominal muscles are relaxed, my heart and lungs are relaxed, my spine is relaxed, my neck and shoulders are relaxed, my brain is relaxed, my eyes are relaxed, my hands and arms are relaxed, my whole being is relaxed, and I feel God's river of peace flowing through me like a golden river of life, love, truth and beauty. The spirit and inspiration of the Almighty flow through me vitalizing, healing and restoring my entire being. The wisdom and power of the Almighty enable me to fulfill all my goals in Divine order through Divine love. I am always relaxed, serene, poised, and balanced, and my faith and confidence is in God and all things good. I can do all things through the God-Power which strengthens me. I dwell in the secret place of the Most High, and all the thoughts entertained by me conform to harmony, peace and goodwill to all. *For God hath not given us the spirit of fear; but of power, and of love, and of a sound mind* (II Timothy 1:7). I sleep in peace and I wake in joy. God supplies all my needs and His riches flow freely into my experience. My security is in God and His love."

He reiterated the above truths frequently during the day, and these wonderful spiritual vibrations neutralized and obliterated the disease-soaked anxiety center in his subconscious mind. His two favorite words became "serenity and tranquility." He discovered there were spiritual reserves on which he could call to annihilate all the anxious and worried thoughts. He now has a deep faith in all things good and has discovered that peace is the power at the heart of God. *And let the peace of God rule in your hearts* (Colossians 3:15).

MEDITATION FOR BEING IN
THE PRESENCE OF INFINITE RICHES

The meditation below has performed wonders for people for richer living and continuing prosperity:

"Today I am reborn spiritually! I completely detach myself from the old way of thinking and I bring Divine love, light and truth definitely into my experience. I consciously feel love for everyone I meet. Mentally I say to everyone I contact, 'I see the God in you and I know you see the God in me.' I recognize the qualities of God in everyone. I practice this morning, noon and night; it is a living part of me.

"I am reborn spiritually now, because all day long I practice the Presence of God. No matter what I am doing — whether I am walking the street, shopping or about my daily business — whenever my thought wanders away from God or the good, I bring it back to the contemplation of His Holy Presence. I feel noble, dignified and God-like. I walk in a high mood sensing my oneness with God. His peace fills my soul."

CHAPTER POINTS TO REMEMBER

1. Nothing can bring you peace but the triumph of principles. Use your mind the right way by feeding it with God-like ideas, and you will experience serenity and tranquility. Think right, feel right, act right, do right and pray right.

2. A certain amount of tension is good. Excess tension is destructive. If you wind your clock too tight, you break the spring. For any important assignment or performance, you accumulate a certain amount of energy, which is the power of God in you enabling you to give a marvelous performance; and like a well-oiled clock, you tick the energy off rhythmically, harmoniously and joyously. Excess tension is fear and anxiety. Contemplate the peace of God flowing through you and the power of the Almighty strengthening you, and the anxiety and fear will be rendered null and void.

3. When you have a lot of unpaid bills, do not dwell on what you owe. Claim God is your instant supply, meeting all your financial needs now. Write down the names of all the creditors and the amounts you owe each one, and give thanks that they are paid in full now. Imagine you are giving each one a check, and that they are smiling and congratulating you. Do it over and over again until you feel the tones of reality.

4. Rejoice and be exceedingly glad in your mind that every creditor is paid now, and that God's wealth is circulating in your life; that you are prospered beyond your fondest dreams. Believe; rejoice; give thanks, for He never faileth.

5. Realize that everything you look at in this universe came out of the invisible mind of God or man. Your thought-image of wealth is first cause relative to that idea in the same way as your radio, motor

car or home are thought-images in the mind of the engineer or builder.

6. No one can disturb you but yourself. It is always the movement of your own thought. It is not what people say or do that annoys you; it is your own reaction or your thought about it. Where there is no opinion, there is no suffering. Keep your eyes on the God-Presence within you and give your allegiance, loyalty and confidence to the Supreme Cause within you. In other words, stop worshipping false gods. With your eyes stayed on God there is no evil on your pathway. God is your boss, your paymaster, your guide and your counsellor, and you give all honor and glory to Him.

7. Excess tension and anxiety interfere with your memory and efficiency along all lines. The ideal way to get a quiet mind is to identify with some of the great eternal truths of the Bible and reiterate these spiritual gems of wisdom. By osmosis, they will penetrate the subconscious mind, and you will find yourself relaxed and at peace. One of these spiritual pearls is: *Thou wilt keep him in perfect peace, whose mind is stayed on thee, because he trusteth in thee* (Isaiah 26:3).

8. When you are tense, anxious, jittery and worried, dwell on this great truth: *For God hath not given us the spirit of fear; but of power, and of love, and of a sound mind* (II Timothy 1:7). If you are an insomniac, affirm prior to sleep: "I sleep in peace, I wake in joy, and I live in God." *When thou liest down, thou shalt not be afraid; yea, thou shalt lie down, and thy sleep shall be sweet.* (Proverbs 3:24).

9. Use the meditation at the end of the chapter to ease tension and anxiety and to realize the God in everyone.

sixteen

How to Automatically Reap an Abundant Harvest of Golden Blessings

The key to self-confidence is given by Emerson in his work on self-reliance: "Trust thyself: every heart vibrates to that iron string . . . Great men have always done so . . . betraying their perception that the absolute trustworthy was seated at their heart, working through their hands, predominating in all thinking."

Great numbers of men and women do not trust themselves; they demean and lower themselves. The real Self of everyone is God, which Emerson refers to as the absolute trustworthy seated in your heart; i.e., the Divine Presence is lodged in your own subjective depths, governing your entire body, watching over you when you are sound asleep. It is the unseen power which moves your hands, and which enables you to walk and talk, revealing to you everything you need to know; and all that is required of you is that you trust this Presence and Power and the answer will be yours. The place of contact and acquaintance is within yourself.

How to Build Self-Confidence

Self-confidence comes when you realize God, which Emerson calls the absolute trustworthy, is in your own subjective depths. Affirm frequently: "God indwells me, walks and talks with me. God is guiding me now. I can do all things through the God-Power which strengthens me. If God be for me, who can be against me? There is no power to challenge God, and God watches over me in all my ways. I realize every problem is Divinely outmatched and I grapple courageously with every assignment, knowing that God reveals the answer. God loves me and cares for me."

Every morning and every evening, become mentally absorbed with the beauty and wisdom of these truths, and gradually they will take possession of you, penetrating your subconscious mind, and you will move through the vicissitudes of life with an abiding faith and confidence, plus a feeling of victory over all problems.

How Self-Confidence Brought a Young Man Riches

While talking with a young pharmacist a few weeks ago, he said to me that two years ago he had been fired from his job for incompetence and that he considered it to be the most fortunate day of his life. He said to himself that only good can come out of this, as "I know that Infinite Intelligence guides, directs and reveals the next step to me." Infinite Intelligence worked wonders for him; he received a deep, intuitive feeling to discuss his dismissal with his father-in-law, who immediately advanced sufficient funds to him to open his own pharmacy, stating that he could gradually pay him back without any interest.

Today he owns two stores and he succeeded in paying back his father-in-law the first year. He believes in the Self within him and in his ability to succeed. His self-confidence has paid him great dividends, not only in money, but in poise, assurance and a rare sense of humor. Remember, self-confidence is contagious; it is communicated subjectively to others, who aid you in the realization of your heart's desire.

His Self-Confidence Dissolved His Lack of Funds

The late Dr. Olive Gaze, an associate of mine, told me about the good fortune of a man who came to her very bitter and hostile to his two brothers, who had cheated him out of a large sum of money. He was in financial straits and somewhat panicky.

She instructed him to place his confidence in the Source and to release his brothers from his hatred as follows: "I surrender my brothers to God completely. I have confidence that God is the eternal Source of my supply. God's love fills my soul. God's peace saturates my mind and heart. I have supreme confidence in God's guidance and directions. I am strong in the Lord and in the power of His might. God's wealth flows to me freely, joyously and endlessly. I give thanks for God's riches now."

As he planted these seeds of love and confidence, all bitterness within him was dissolved. He had been taking care of his grandmother, who was very old and feeble and did not want to go to a retirement home. He visited her twice a day and saw to it that she was provided for. He got her groceries, paid her bills and drove her to church on Sundays, all the time thinking that she was living on a meager pension plus social security. He was motivated by kindness and love; he did not expect or look for any reward.

His grandmother passed on suddenly one evening, however, and imagine his surprise when an attorney called him and informed him that her entire estate had been bequeathed to him. This estate was worth $150,000, three times the amount he was cheated out of by his brothers. His confidence in the Source of all blessings, plus his giving of love, forgiveness and goodwill, brought him an abundant harvest.

Building Self-Confidence Prior to Going to Sleep

One of the most powerful ways to develop self-confidence is prior to sleep when you are in a sleepy, drowsy, relaxed state. Then there is an outcropping of your subconscious mind, and that is one of the best times to instill new ideas which impregnate your deeper mind. During the sleep period, these ideas gestate in the darkness of your mind, and your deeper mind determines the best way to bring riches, prosperity and success to you.

A businessman said to me that he was plagued with the fear of failure and bankruptcy and that he was unable to pay the bills of his wholesaler. Accordingly, I gave him the following thoughts of confidence, wealth and success to be affirmed slowly, quietly and feelingly every night prior to sleep. The formula was as follows:

"I sleep in peace every night and I wake in joy and confidence, knowing that God is guiding me and reveals the perfect plan for the fulfillment of my desires. My business is God's business, and God's business always prospers. God's wealth circulates in my life and there is always a surplus. I am consistently attracting to me more and more customers, and every day of my life I am giving greater service. All my employees are blessed and prospered, and happiness, prosperity and the riches of God reign supreme in the minds and hearts of all. I am full of confidence and absolute trust in my senior partner, which is God."

The businessman practiced this prayer-therapy technique every night, and as he charged his subconscious with these life-giving patterns, he found his whole life and business patterns changing. A chain store offered him a wonderful price for his store and lot in order to build a new branch there. He was delighted to sell and received far more than he anticipated, enabling him to pay up all his debts and retire to Hawaii, where he and his wife bought a condominium and in the future plan to do extensive travelling. All his employees were absorbed by the chain store.

The ways of your Divine inner mind are past finding out. He proved to himself that his subconscious was a real bank with money in it for him which magnifies exceedingly that which he deposits in it.

The Riches of a New Estimate of Yourself

Approve of yourself, accept yourself, realizing you are an individualized expression of God. You are a son or daughter of the Living God. Remember your new estimate or blueprint is your deep conviction in the Supreme Intelligence within you, which always responds to your thought. Place your faith in that which never changes but which is the same yesterday, today and forever. Theologies, governments, philosophies, and fiscal values wax and wane; floods come and go; everything changes and passes away in this universe. But remember, when you place your confidence in the Life-Principle within you, you will never want for any good thing, and whatever form money takes, you will always have all you need as well as a Divine surplus.

Remember the great truths: *I will fear no evil: for thou art with me* (Psalm 23:4) *For he shall give his angels charge over thee, to keep thee in all thy ways* (Psalm 91:11).

She Found the Riches of Self-Confidence Dissolved Her Inferiority Complex

A young lady in a department store said to me, "I am nobody. I was born on the wrong side of the tracks. I did not get a good education." I explained to her that she could completely banish all sense of inferiority and self-rejection by changing her concept of herself and by knowing that conditions, experiences and events in her life were effects, not causatives.

She decided to banish all sense of inferiority by realizing the following truths: "I am a daughter of God. I am unique; there is no one in all the world like me, because God never repeats Himself. God is my Father and I am His child. God loves me and cares for me. Any time I am prone to criticize or find fault with myself, I will immediately affirm: 'I exalt God in the midst of me.' God is now expressing Himself in a wonderful way through me. I radiate love, peace and goodwill to all. I am one with my Father, and my

Father is God. I know the real Self of me is God, and from this moment forward, I have a healthy, reverent respect for the Divinity within me, which created me and gave me life, breath and all things."

As she meditated on these truths, she found all sense of insecurity and inferiority vanish. She began to think quietly of the kind of husband she would like to marry. She became acquainted shortly thereafter with a customer in the store who was the answer to her mental dreams. All this happened within a month's time. She found herself lifted out of a humdrum life, married, with a sumptuous home and a devoted husband. She found the riches within first, and then found the riches of life on the screen of space.

Benefits of Practicing the Riches of Praise

A young man came to me saying that his professor suggested that he join a class in calculus, but he said that he was afraid to do so; that he didn't know enough. I explained to him by saying, "Robby, the professor would not have asked you if he did not have confidence and trust in your ability. Furthermore, Infinite Intelligence is within you and you are wise enough and smart enough to know that It always responds to you. You have what it takes. You are alert, smart, on the *qui vive,* you have a brilliant mind, and you have great faith in God and His laws of mind. I have perfect confidence that you can do it, and I want you to accept the offer at once. God will guide you in your studies and reveal to you everything you need to know."

This was the essence of what I said to Robby. He beamed with delight at my confidence in him and my praise of his mental acumen and sagacity, and today he is the top man in his calculus class. He was made president of his class and is a confidant of the professor of mathematics.

What Robby needed was someone to stir up his confidence and appreciation of his Higher Self. Remember, wholesouled confidence in the Self of you and that of others will bring about miracles in your life and also in their lives.

A Wife Discovers the Riches of Calling Forth Confidence in Her Husband

The wife of a college instructor said to me that her husband was extraordinarily brilliant but that he seemed to have no ambition; that he had not been promoted in three years. She added, "I think he feels inferior and inadequate."

I suggested that instead of talking to him, which she had tried in vain to do, that she practice instead the silent method, which she accomplished as follows. About three times a day for about three or four minutes each time, she would affirm the following, knowing that he would receive her affirmations subjectively, and that his subconscious mind would compel him to express his latent powers and abilities.

"My husband is a tremendous success. He is absolutely outstanding. The Infinite within him is all-wise and all-powerful. My husband is going from glory to glory; he is going up the ladder of success and promotion. His real talents are revealed and appreciated. He is Divinely guided and his success comes to pass now. I give thanks, for I know what I decree stirs up the gift of God within him."

Within three months' time, he was promoted to associate professor. He also became a consultant to a large corporation and his income has trebled. He is fulfilling her conviction for his success, including financial success.

MEDITATION FOR BUILDING SELF-CONFIDENCE

"I know that the answer to my problem lies in the God-Self within me. I now get quiet, still and relaxed. I am at peace. I know God speaks in peace and not in confusion. I am now in tune with the Infinite; I know and believe implicitly that Infinite Intelligence is revealing to me the perfect answer. I think about the solution to my problems. I now live in the mood I would have were my problem solved. I truly live in this abiding faith and trust which is the mood of the solution; this is the spirit of God moving within me. This Spirit is Omnipotent; It is manifesting Itself; my whole being rejoices in the solution; I am glad. I live in this feeling and give thanks.

"I know that God has the answer. With God all things are possible. God is the Living Spirit Almighty within me; He is the source of all wisdom and illumination.

"The indicator of the Presence of God within me is a sense of peace and poise. I now cease all sense of strain and struggle; I trust the God-Power implicitly. I know that all the Wisdom and Power I need to live a glorious and successful life are within me. I relax my entire body; my faith is in His Wisdom; I go free. I claim and feel the peace of God flooding my mind, heart and whole being. I know the quiet mind gets its problems solved. I now turn the request over to the God-Presence knowing It has an answer. I am at peace."

CHAPTER POINTS TO REMEMBER

1. Emerson said, "Trust thyself; every heart vibrates to that iron string. The absolutely trustworthy is seated in your own heart." To know that God indwells you, walks and talks in you and responds to your thoughts gives you confidence and faith in that which never fails.

2. You build self-confidence by knowing that the God-Power in you is almighty. There is nothing to oppose omnipotence, nothing to challenge it, and when your thoughts are God's thoughts, God's power is with your thoughts of good. Realize that God loves you and cares for you, and then all sense of insecurity and fear goes away.

3. When you are fired from a position, don't get depressed or angry, but realize the God-Presence within you will open up a new door of expression for you in Divine order and you will experience the joy of the answered prayer.

4. Place your confidence in God, the Source of all blessings. As you call upon It, the answer comes.

Claim, "God's wealth is circulating in my life and God is guiding me." If resentment is present toward any person, release that person, wishing for him or her all the blessings of life. As you fill your mind and heart with Divine love, all bitterness and resentment is dissolved and your good will flow to you.

5. Practice conveying ideas of prosperity, success, and wealth to your subconscious prior to sleep. As you make a habit of this, you will establish patterns of wealth and success in your life, and the powers of your subconscious being compulsive, you will find yourself compelled to express the riches of God along all lines. You will find that unseen forces hasten to minister to your eternal good.

6. Approve of yourself. You are a child of the Infinite and heir to all the riches of life. The Self of you is God. Honor and exalt the God-Presence within you. Know, believe and practice aligning yourself mentally with the God-Presence within you, knowing that It will respond to you and take care of you all the days of your life. You will experience riches and peace in this changing world.

7. All inferiority disappears as you contemplate that God is your Father and that He loves you and cares for you. Whenever you're prone to denigrate or demean yourself, affirm: "I exalt God in the midst of me." As you make a habit of this, all sense of self-rejection and inferiority disappears. As you practice this technique, God will flow through you, filling up all the empty vessels in your life.

8. As you praise the qualities, powers, talents and abilities in others, they will rise to the occasion and you will find that they really stir up the gifts of God within them. Praise is a miracle-working power. Practice it.

9. If married, you can convey the riches of silent praise to your husband or wife. There is no time or space

in mind, and as you affirm with feeling and understanding that your partner is a tremendous success,
Divinely guided, and Divinely expressed, and Divinely prospered in all ways, your beliefs will be conveyed to your partner subconsciously and your
partner will fulfill your conviction of him or her.
What you decree shall come to pass. Paul says:
"Therefore, I put thee in remembrance that thou
stir up the gift of God within thee."
10. Use the meditation at the end of the chapter to
attain the peace and quiet of self-confidence.

seventeen

How to Call Upon the Healing Presence to Bring the Riches You Want

There is one Universal Healing Power. It is omnipotent; it is in the soil, the cat, the dog and the tree. It is called by many names, such as the Infinite Healing Presence, God, Allah, the One Soul, Divine Providence, Nature, and Life and the Life Principle, as well as many others. The awareness of the Infinite Healing Presence is lost in the night of time by the average person. Over the ancient temples were written these words: "The doctor dresses the wound, and God heals the patient."

This marvelous healing power resides in your own subconscious mind, which is the maker of your body. This healing power will heal a sick financial condition, a broken home, a disease-wracked body, marital discord and emotional distress and troubles of all kinds. You will remember when you were young how this healing presence brought curative results to your burns, cuts, bruises, contusions and sprains; and probably, in your youth, like the author, you did not aid the healing process in any way by the application of such topical remedies as mercurochrome, Friar's balsam, tincture of iodine, and so on.

How a Mother Applied the Riches of the Healing Presence

A young woman working in a department store and earning her own living became engaged to be married to a very fine young man, but he was of a different religious belief, and her mother, who was very domineering and possessive, sought by every means possible to break up the romance, even to the point of openly insulting the young man, calling him a "foreigner," a heathen and unfit for her daughter. She was actually trying to force her daughter into another decision, against the daughter's better judgment.

This young woman deeply resented her mother's interference and willfulness; however, she repressed her hostility and resentment. She eventually suffered a nervous breakdown and was confined to the hospital for some weeks. She was placed on tranquilizers, but when the effect of the drugs wore off, the psychic infection of hostility and suppressed rage remained present.

On visiting her at the hospital, I explained to her that she was an adult and should come to her own decision and refuse to be influenced by anybody; that love knows no creed, race or color, as love transcends all these things. I said to her, "The minute you come to a decision and marry the man of your dreams, whom you love, a healing will come." I suggested to the young man that he should visit her, which he did. They agreed to get married irrespective of what her mother said or didn't say.

I performed the ceremony, and she now has a remarkable sense of freedom and peace of mind. After the ceremony, she phoned her mother and told her that she had been married and was on her way to Europe. Her mother fumed, but the daughter said: "Mother, I have released you to God. You no longer dictate to me: neither do you manipulate my mind anymore. Goodbye and God bless you. From now on, I seek guidance from On High, and His wisdom and love will lead me to ways of pleasantness and paths of peace."

Recently I had a card from this young lady, and she is now living in Argentina. Her husband has inherited a vast ranch, and they are immensely happy and experiencing the riches of life. Her mother later sought counsel from me and there has developed a marvelous *rapprochement* with her daughter. Love pays fabulous dividends.

How to Apply the Healing Power of Freedom

A woman consulted me, stating that she was terribly worried about her son; that he and his wife were quarreling and that the children were not being brought up right. I asked her how old her son was, and she said he was fifty-five years old. She was also worried about the company he kept, as he frequented bars.

I explained to her that she should never interfere with her son's marital problems and that she should immediately cease thinking that he should do what she wanted him to do, or that he should act the way she thinks he should act, or believe the way she thinks he should believe. I suggested to her that she release him, set him free and get her own mind in order and at peace.

I wrote out this prayer for her: "I surrender my son, his wife and family to God completely, lock, stock and barrel. I loose them and let them go. I give him freedom to lead his own life in his own way, knowing that he is God's man and that God loves him and cares for him and his family. I release him and set him free spiritually, mentally and emotionally. Any time he, his wife or family come to my mind, I will immediately affirm, 'I have released you. God be with you. I am free now and so are you.' It is God in action in my life, which means harmony, peace and right action."

She practiced this prayer therapy faithfully and found

an inner sense of peace and tranquility which she had hither-to not known. She discovered a simple truth: when we set others free and release them to God's guidance and direction, we are set free ourselves.

Exalt the Divinity in your loved ones and friends and permit them to discover the Divinity which shapes their ends. Never try to bend them to your will or your own preconceived opinions and beliefs. Allow the other to succeed or fail, and if he fails, it may well be the turning point of his life, whereby he discovers the power that never fails deep within himself — the Infinite which lies stretched in smiling repose. In this way, you discover the riches of freedom.

How a Businessman Discovered the Riches of Surrender

An emotionally-wracked and distraught businessman consulted me, stating that he wanted a prayer to use to get his wife back. She had divorced him in another state. They had been married twenty years. He said that he had come home one night and found a note, which said that she was leaving to obtain a divorce. She had given no further explanation and he had no idea where she had gone. This man apparently wanted to mentally coerce his wife to return to him.

I explained to him that it is always wrong to try to force, mentally coerce or try to influence another in any way to do one's bidding; that he should not want a woman who didn't want him. He should grant her the right ot make her own decisions, and what is Divine guidance for one is guidance for the other. To say that she suddenly left without any reason is simply not true. She must have been thinking of running away and imaging life elsewhere for a long time. Finally, her mental image became subjectified, and the nature of her subconscious being compulsive, it caused her to pack up and leave. But she had been leaving mentally for a long time.

Accordingly, I gave him a pattern of prayer to follow:

I surrender my wife to God completely. I know Infinite Intelligence leads and guides her in all ways. Divine right action reigns supreme. I know that what is right action for her is also right action for me. I give her complete freedom, because I know that love frees, it gives, it is the spirit of God. There are harmony, peace and understanding between us. I wish for her all the blessings of life. I loose her and let her go."

In talking to this man, I discovered that he had been very jealous of his wife, and very possessive and domineering, restricting her activities to the house only. She resented this domination and undoubtedly decided to leave, and for a period of time had mentally lived elsewhere. When your body is in one place and in your imagination your mind is elsewhere, you will be eventually compelled to go where your vision is. If a spouse is suffering from suppressed rage and resentment, the result may be involvement with someone else, or it may turn to sickness and mental aberrations of all kinds. Love is not possessiveness. Love is not jealousy. Love is not domineering or coercive. When you love another, you love to see the other happy, joyous and free. Love is freedom.

This man listened carefully. To understand all is to forgive all. He practiced his prayer therapy, and in a month's time, his wife wrote him from Mexico, where she had filed for a divorce. She later married a man from South America and is apparently very happy. She wrote him a very kind letter and told him why she had left, which coincided with what is written here.

Infinite Intelligence is all-wise, and when you pray for guidance and right action, you do not tell the Infinite its business. He was at peace about the whole matter and prayed for a Divine companion; he eventually married a young lady he had met at one of my lectures. They blend and harmonize perfectly. He is a changed man. He handled the matter correctly and the law of love gave him peace, tranquility and a lovely wife. Love is the fulfilling of the law of health, happiness, prosperity and peace of mind.

How a Nurse Received a Quarter of a Million Dollars Through the Riches of the Healing Presence

On the plane to Mexico City, a registered nurse sat next to me and we began to talk. She was from New York, and she told me that she had been invited to teach in one of the hospitals in Mexico. She had been married for five years, when one day her husband asked her for a divorce, saying he was in love with another woman. She said, "I told him that he was as free as the wind; that I wanted him to be happy." She said to me, "I go to a metaphysical church in New York, and I know that love always frees. My husband was surprised that I wasn't angry or bitter, so I explained to him that love is never possessive; love wants the other to be happy, and I told my husband, 'by freeing you I set myself free.'"

He got his divorce and married the other woman. She died in a year's time though, and a year later he passed on of a coronary attack. He left his entire estate to the nurse which totalled a quarter of a million dollars. She had set him free and wished for him all the blessings of life, and her love and goodwill came back to her a hundred hundredfold !

How a Junior Executive Built His Promotions

While talking to a junior executive in San Diego where I was giving some lectures, he revealed that he had been passed up for four consecutive years but that other junior executives had been promoted, and he thought it was unfair. In talking to him, I discovered that he really expected to be passed over and, like Job of old: *The thing I greatly feared is come upon me* (Job 3:25).

He learned that promotion and demotion take place in his own mind and that, actually, he gives everything to himself. His superiors bore testimony to his belief about himself. Man's belief is always made manifest whether he is consciously thinking about it or not.

At my suggestion he changed his mental attitude and began to affirm regularly and systematically: "Promotion is mine, success is mine, wealth is mine, Divine right action is mine." As he continued to claim these truths, he activated the latent powers of his subconscious, and since the law of his subconscious is compulsive, at the end of three months he became the chief executive, with his income doubled at the same time. He was healed of a false belief, and in his phone call to me, he said, "It is true. I promoted myself."

How the Riches of the Healing Presence
Worked for All in an Office

In San Diego at the Royal Inn Hotel, overlooking the beautiful harbor full of ships from many foreign nations, I set aside a day for interviews. One of the most interesting was a visit from a talented young lady who was working in an office with twenty other girls, most of whom were very critical of the management, and terribly dissatisfied and disgruntled. The coffee breaks consisted mostly of negative talk about their husbands, their ailments and the low pay they were receiving. She said to me that she liked her work and the pay and that her boss was very kind, sincere and most understanding, but that she was constantly bombarded by the negative thoughts around her, and she felt depressed and dejected at the end of the day.

At my suggestion, she wrote down the names of the twenty girls, and night and morning she prayed for them as follows: "All these girls are known in Divine Mind. They are in their true place, doing what they love to do, and are Divinely happy and Divinely prospered. God thinks, speaks and acts through them. They are conscious of their true worth and they are experiencing spiritual, mental and material riches now. I loose them and let them go, and whenever I hear any negative statement from any one of them, I will immediately affirm, 'God loves you and cares for you.'"

Within three weeks or so, many of the girls had resigned for better positions, some got married, some were transferred to better-paying positions in the organization, one employee married the vice-president, and the girl whom I counselled married the young president of the corporation. All of them were blessed, and the new crew in her office were constructive thinkers and students of the Science of Mind. She discovered that by blessing others, she not only contributed to their good, but the blessing also came back to her pressed down, shaken together and running over.

How Parents Found the Riches of
Releasing Their Daughter to a New Normal Life

The parents of a girl visited me here at the Royal Inn in San Diego. They were overwrought and emotionally wracked over their daughter, who suddenly left college in the East and went to Hawaii with some young people they called "hippies." She wrote them from the Island of Maui and said that she was sleeping on the beach with others and that she liked the life. She demanded money to be sent to the local post office, general delivery. The parents were incensed, terribly angry; and the father said, "I won't give her a dime."

My suggestion to them was along the following lines. She is twenty-one years old. She is an adult and has to live her own life without dictation from her parents. I also said that it is morally, ethically and spiritually wrong to contribute to the delinquency, laziness, apathy and sloth of another person, as they become leaners and whiners; furthermore, financial help too frequently and easily given robs the other of self-propulsion, incentive and initiative.

They agreed to release their daughter completely, knowing that the Infinite Healing Presence would take care of their daughter in the right way, provided they used the law of mind in the right way.

The prayer therapy technique I outlined for them was as follows: "I release my daughter to God completely. She is a daughter of God, and God loves her and cares for her. God is guiding her, and Divine law and order govern her entire life. Whenever we think of her, we will immediately affirm, 'God is watching over you and He careth for you.'"

Six weeks passed by and they heard nothing from their daughter, but they sent no money. They just prayed night and morning for her, as outlined in this chapter. On the seventh week they had a letter from her, saying that she was a waitress at night in one of the hotels and had enrolled in the University of Hawaii and intended to graduate. She apologized for her actions in leaving the college in the East and for her waywardness and asked forgiveness.

The parents phoned me and said they were going to Hawaii to see her and there was a joyous reunion. They discovered the riches of releasing their daughter to the care of the Infinite, which knows all and sees all. Its ways are pleasantness and its paths are peace.

MEDITATION FOR APPLYING THE HEALING PRINCIPLE

"'I will restore health unto thee, and I will heal thee of thy wounds, saith the Lord.' The God in me has limitless possibilities. I know that all things are possible with God. I believe this and accept it wholeheartedly now. I know that the God-Power in me makes darkness light and crooked things straight. I am now lifted up in consciousness by contemplating that God indwells me.

"I speak the word now for the healing of mind, body and affairs; I know that this Principle within me responds to my faith and trust. 'The Father doeth the works.' I am now in touch with life, love, truth and beauty within me. I now align myself with the Infinite Principle of Love and Life within me. I know that harmony, health and peace are now being expressed in my body.

"As I live, move and act in the assumption of my perfect health, it becomes actual. I now imagine and feel the reality of my perfect body. I am filled with a sense of peace and well being. Thank you, Father."

CHAPTER POINTS TO REMEMBER

1. The Infinite Healing Presence is present everywhere. This Healing Presence heals a cut on your finger, reduces the edema in a burn and restores your skin to a normal condition. It will also heal marital problems and financial troubles. It is the solution to all problems.

2. Parents should never interfere with the choice of a spouse selected by a daughter or son. The daughter or son, as the case may be, should be free to make his or her own decision, and the parents should simply release their offspring to God, knowing that Infinite Intelligence guides and directs the young person, and that Divine right action prevails.

3. It is foolish to insist that your married sons or daughters should conform to your way of thinking, acting and believing. Release your son to God, wishing for him all the blessings of life. Loose him and let him go. Where there is no opinion, there is no suffering. Whenever you think of a loved one, affirm: "I have released you. God be with you." When you do this, you set yourself free.

4. If your wife packs up and leaves you, that is her decision. It is wrong for a husband to try to mentally coerce or force his wife to return. He should use the spiritual law by realizing Infinite Intelligence is guiding and directing her in all ways, knowing that what is Divine guidance for her is also guidance for him and for everybody in the world. Give her Divine freedom, knowing that Divine right action prevails; then whatever happens blesses all. Love is not possessiveness. Love frees, it gives; it is the spirit of God.

5. Love always frees. Love is not possessiveness. When you love another, whether wife or husband, you love to see the other happy, joyous and free. You love to see the other as the other ought to be. If your spouse falls madly in love with another, release her or him and wish for your spouse all the blessings of life. Love frees.

6. You will discover that if you expect to be overlooked for promotion or advancement, your subconscious accepts your belief as a request and sees to it that you are passed over. You promote yourself, for according to your belief is it done unto you. Promotion takes place in your own mind. Affirm regularly: "Promotion is mine, success is mine, wealth is mine, right action is mine." Lull yourself to sleep with these truths and your subconscious will respond and compel you to rise higher and prosper along all lines.

7. When others are talking negatively in your office and recounting all their pains, aches and troubles, surrender all of them to God, knowing that God thinks, speaks and acts through them and that they are Divinely led to their true expression in life. In other words, radiate love, peace and goodwill to them, and you will set the wonders of your prayer in action. They will be blessed and so will you. You will discover that by exalting God in others, you also will bring countless blessings to yourself.

8. When your daughter is of age, loose her and let her go. Claim that God is guiding her and that she is in His care, and as you remain faithful to that prayer, your daughter will pick it up subjectively and be Divinely led to do the right thing. Be patient, trust the Infinite Intelligence within you, and don't argue in your mind. Infinite Intelligence knows all and sees all. All that is required of you is to trust and believe, and it is done unto you as you believe.

9. Apply the meditation at the end of the chapter for amazing benefits of the Healing Presence in your daily living.

eighteen

How to Use Mind-Magic to Make Riches Flow

A few weeks ago I attended a religious convention at Airlie, near Washington, D.C., where I spoke on the topic, "Law Which Never Changes." During the five days I was there, I had a long talk with a very successful and immensely wealthy man, who told me that the secret of his health, wealth and outstanding achievement was in the developing of what he called the "quiet mind."

He had a card in his pocket on which the following great truths were inscribed: "The superior man is always quiet and calm" (Confucius). *In quietness and in confidence shall be your strength (Isaiah 30:15). He that is slow to anger is better than the mighty; and he that ruleth his spirit than he that taketh a city (Proverbs 16:32). The Lord thy God shall bless thee in all thine increase, and in all the works of thine hands, therefore thou shalt surely rejoice (Deuteronomy 16:15). Except the Lord build the house, they labour in vain that build it (Psalm 127:1).*

All these statements point out that your strength, success, power and riches come from serenity, from the inner peace of quietness and from confidence in the laws of life and the response of your subconscious mind.

How This Rich Man Used These Truths

This man said that every morning of his life he anchored his mind on the above-mentioned truths, repeating them slowly, quietly and lovingly, knowing that as they were impressed in his subconscious mind, he would be compelled to express success, health, vitality and new creative ideas. He has established four large corporations and is advisor to many executives in different fields. He travels the world over.

He said to me while presenting me with one of his meditation cards, which he dispenses freely, that thirty years ago he met a man on a ship to Europe who explained to him that if he took certain constructive words from the Bible — words which represent the eternal truths of God and His Law — his mind would become anchored on the Supreme Presence, which responds as you call upon It.

The whole key to his riches was that he knew as he meditated on the above-mentioned Biblical phrases regularly, systematically and repetitiously that he was activating the latent power within his subliminal depths, compelling him to move onward, upward and Godward.

A Businessman Discovers the Riches of the Silence

Carlyle said, "Silence is the element in which great things fashion themselves." Emerson said, "Let us be silent that we may hear the whispers of the gods."

A prominent businessman told me that he attributes all his successful business decisions to fifteen-minute silent periods in the mornings. He withdraws his attention and sensory awareness from the external world, quiets his body, closes his eyes and contemplates the great truth that Infinite Intelligence is within him. Silently, he affirms that God is guiding him; that new, creative ideas are given to him; that the Divine Presence will govern the conferences of the day; that God thinks, speaks and acts through him; that the right words are given to him by the Supreme Wisdom within him; and that all decisions for his company are based on right action, blessing all.

He then spends about five minutes in what he calls transcendental meditation by simply imagining God's river of peace flowing through his whole being. Ofttimes, while in this quiet period, solutions to acute business and personnel problems pop into his mind — problems with which he and other associates had been struggling for days.

How to "Get the Answers"

He states he has discovered that the quickest way in all the world to get an answer to a problem is to turn over your request to that center of quietness, knowing the answer will emerge. Many times the answer comes within an hour, although the answer may come a few days later, or perhaps a week later, but it always comes when he is preoccupied with something else. Apparently his subconscious mind gathers all the material necessary and then, at the right time, presents it full-blown to his conscious, reasoning mind. Some of the ideas which are resurrected are worth a small fortune. One of his recent ideas emerging from his quiet period was worth over $200,000.

How a Woman Received a Marvelous Answer in the Quiet Period Concerning Her Possible Marriage

Every Sunday we open with a quiet period, a directed silence wherein all are instructed not to take their problems into the Higher Self within, which knows only the answer, but, on the other hand, to contemplate the answer, the solution, the creative ideas, the way out welling up from their subjective depths. I point out that there are creative answers in their subconscious minds that could and would revolutionize their entire lives.

Last Sunday, a woman said to me, "All of a sudden, I saw a scene in my mind's eye of the man I was about to marry. He was with his wife and his two children. Intuitively, I knew it was his wife. I had been in doubt and was hesitating about the marriage. I received my answer, and when talking to him later about what I had experienced in silence at the Wilshire Ebell Theatre, he admitted that he was not divorced and was about to marry me just for my money."

They parted in peace. She gave him a book to read, *The Secrets of the I Ching,*[1] which he subsequently told her had transformed his whole life.

How a Quiet Mind Dissolved Destructive Criticism

A young woman in charge of a very large department employing a great number of girls told me that she is subject to a great deal of criticism and backbiting, but takes it all philosophically by following the injunction of the Bible: *When he giveth quietness, who then can make trouble?* (Job 34:29). She said, "I join up with the God-Presence within me, realizing no one can hurt me, as 'one with God is a majority.' Moreover, I realize that if some girl is jealous and speaks ill of me, she cannot hurt me because I know that negative thoughts and statements of others have no power to create the things they suggest, and I refuse to transfer the power within me to others. My thought is creative. My thoughts are God's thoughts, and God's power is with my thoughts of good."

She is a wise young woman. She knows that no matter what lies others may spread about her, they cannot hurt her unless she accepts the thought mentally. Because others speak ill of you does not make it so. Your thought is creative, and you are the master of your own mind and should positively refuse to let others disturb you or manipulate your mind.

---

[1]See *The Secrets of the I Ching,* by Dr. Joseph Murphy, Parker Publishing Company, Inc., West Nyack, New York, 1970.

There is an old German proverb: "A lie cannot go very far, for it has short legs."

Her philosophy is simple and to the point in that she said that if some girl points a finger of criticism at her, the girl's other three fingers are pointing toward herself. It is as simple as that.

The Riches of the Quiet Mind Induce Sleep for a Chronic Insomnia Sufferer

I gave the following formula to a businesswoman who said she had to take two sleeping tablets every night because she was so tense and keyed up: "In bed, talk to your body as follows: My toes are relaxed, my ankles are relaxed, my feet are relaxed, my legs are relaxed, my abdominal muscles are relaxed, my heart and lungs are relaxed, my spine is relaxed, my hands and arms are relaxed, my shoulders are relaxed, my neck is relaxed, my brain is relaxed, my eyes are relaxed, my facial muscles are relaxed. I now feel God's river of peace flowing through me, permeating every atom of my being. I sleep in peace; I wake in joy."

She quietly repeated these simple truths every night, knowing her body is subject to her thoughts, and after a week or so of practicing this discipline, she has had no further trouble. She has discovered the meaning of these great truths: *Acquaint now thyself with Him and be at peace* (Job 22:21). *Casting all your care upon him, for he careth for you* (I Peter 5:7).

How a Tense and Anxious Executive Discovered the Riches of Healing Passages of the Bible

Recently I talked with an executive who said to me, "My problem is extreme tension and anxiety about every decision I have to make." Accordingly, I gave him what I call a spiritual prescription which would bring peace to his troubled mind. I suggested to him that as he used the following spiritual truths by affirming them quietly, feelingly and knowingly, his excess tension would gradually abate:

Thou wilt keep him in perfect peace, whose mind is stayed on thee, because he trusteth in thee (Isaiah 26:3). *In quietness and confidence shall be your strength* (Isaiah 30:15). *But my God shall supply all your need according to his riches in glory* (Philippians 4:19). *Acquaint now thyself with him, and be at peace: thereby good shall come unto thee* (Job 22:21). *Casting all your care upon him; for he careth for you* (I Peter 5:7). *When he giveth quietness, who then can make trouble?* (Job 34:29).

This executive affirmed these healing, therapeutic passages of scripture several times daily, spending five or ten minutes at each quiet session, and he found composure, peace, serenity and mind control. He discovered that peace is the power at the heart of God.

A Salesman Discovers the Secret of Increased Sales in Riches of a Quiet Mind

Marcus Aurelius, the wise Roman Emperor, said: "A man's life is dyed by the color of his imagination." In talking to a salesman the other day, I learned that he was very apprehensive and worried over what he called a "nut letter" from his sales manager, criticizing him for his low sales.

I suggested to him that night and morning he read the 23rd Psalm, which would quiet his mind. I suggested that his faculty of using his imagination constructively would transform his life. Imagination is the art of projecting images, the discipline of mental images.

This salesman reversed the mental picture of poor sales and failure. Morning and night for five or ten minutes, after reading out loud the 23rd Psalm, he imagined his sales manager in front of him, congratulating him on his excellent sales. He felt the naturalness of his handshake. He clearly heard his voice, saw his smile, and heard him say over and over again, "Congratulations on your splendid performance.

You are being promoted to a higher echelon in the corporation." He lulled himself to sleep every night operating that mental movie.

He found his sales improving. He also took a course in public speaking, and at the end of three months he was made district manager, receiving a wonderful increase in salary and commissions. He is on the way to the top. By repeating the mental movie night and morning in a quiet, passive, receptive way, he implanted the idea of promotion and advancement in his subconscious mind, and the latter opened up the way for the perfect manifestation of the impression he made on his deeper mind.

How the Riches of Quiet Understanding
Healed a Threatened Mental Crack-Up

One day a man from San Francisco flew down to see me. He was extremely tense. His doctor had diagnosed his condition as anxiety neurosis, which is another name for chronic worry and excess tension. He was very successful financially and was sales manager of a very big corporation. He was very well liked by the president and vice-president of the corporation.

As I talked with him, the root, or real cause of his trouble, came to light. A classmate of his was sales manager of a rival corporation but had been promoted to the position of president of the corporation. He admitted that he was jealous and envious of his classmate's promotion. He was mentally competing with him. He said, "You know, that fellow beat me at everything in school and college; he even took away the girl I loved and married her."

I explained to him that the only true competition there was in life was that which existed between the idea of success and the idea of failure in his own mind and that he was born to win, not fail; for the Infinite could not fail. Therefore, all he had to do was to focus his attention on success and then all the powers of his subconscious would back him up and compel him to succeed, as the law of the subconscious is compulsive.

He began to see that the past is dead and that nothing matters but this moment. As he changed his present thoughts and kept them changed, his whole world would magically melt into the image and likeness of his contemplation.

I also explained to him that by entertaining envious thoughts, he was actually impoverishing himself and that this was one of the worst possible attitudes to hold, because his negative thinking and his feeling of inferiority plus envy and jealousy were playing havoc with his mental and emotional life and would tend to block his expansion along all lines.

The Simple Remedy

The remedy was very simple. He decided to bless and sincerely wish greater prosperity and success for his former classmate, whose apparently more successful and prosperous state had incited him to envy. Accordingly, he prayed frequently as follows: "I recognize God as my instant and everlasting supply. Promotion is mine in Divine order. Success is mine in Divine order. God's wealth flows to me in avalanches of abundance, and I am Divinely guided to give better service every day. I know, believe and rejoice that God is prospering my former classmate, and I sincerely wish for him all the blessings of life. Whenever he comes to my mind, I will immediately affirm, 'God multiplies your good.'"

After a few weeks, he discovered that the envious thoughts lost all momentum, and he found that the cause of his anxiety and excess tension had been due entirely to his state of mind. This young man has been promoted recently to executive vice-president and undoubtedly is on the way to the top. The Bible says: *If thou return to the Almighty, thou shalt be built up* (Job 22:23).

By blessing those whose promotion, success and wealth annoy us or incite our envy or jealousy, and by wishing that they become even more prosperous and more successful in every way, we heal our own minds and open the door to the riches of the Infinite. Out of the abundance of your heart you can pour out the gifts of praise, love, joy and laughter. You can give a transfusion of courage, faith and confidence to all those around you, and you will discover that by blessing others, you, too, will be blessed, and all sense of envy, inferiority and lack will be overcome.

A College Student Discovers the Riches of the Quiet Mind

A fourth-year medical student said to me, "I'm haunted by a shadowy, pervasive anxiety day and night, a fear of failure and apprehension about the future." He said that in one examination his mind went blank and he could only answer a few of the questions. This young man's trouble was anxiety and worry. He was afraid of oral and written examinations and was giving the worry orders to his subconscious mind. He developed stress, which brought about a mental block.

I suggested that every night prior to sleep, he should affirm slowly and quietly, "I am relaxed, at peace, serene and calm. I have a perfect memory for everything I need to know at every moment of time and point of space. I am Divinely guided in my studies and I am completely relaxed and at peace at all examinations. I pass all my examinations in Divine order, and I sleep in peace and I wake in joy."

I explained to him that all these ideas would sink deeply into his subconscious mind, becoming a part of him, so that either in an oral or a written examination he would give an excellent account of himself.

At last report, he is doing splendidly. His anxiety has been lifted and his latent abilities and memory of all he learned were set free. *In quietness and in confidence shall be your strength* (Isaiah 30:15).

MEDITATION FOR THE RICHES OF THE QUIET MIND

The following meditation repeated often can bring you your heart's desires in unexpected ways:

"'Those that be planted in the house of the Lord shall flourish in the courts of our God.' I am still and at peace. My heart and my mind are motivated by the spirit of goodness, truth and beauty. My thought is now on the Presence of God within me; this stills my mind.

"I know that the way of creation is Spirit moving upon Itself. My True Self now moves in and on Itself creating peace, harmony and health in my body and affairs. I am Divine in my deeper self. I know I am a son of the living God; I create the way God creates by the self-contemplation of spirit. I know my body does not move of itself. It is acted upon by my thoughts and emotions.

"I now say to my body, 'Be still and quiet.' It must obey. I understand this and I know it is a Divine Law. I take my attention away from the physical world; I feast in the House of God within me. I meditate and feast upon harmony, health and peace; these come forth from the God-Essence within; I am at peace. My body is a temple of the Living God. 'God is in His Holy Temple; let all the earth keep silent before Him.'"

CHAPTER POINTS TO REMEMBER

1. Confucious said: "The superior man is always quiet and calm." The Bible says: *In quietness and in confidence shall be your strength* (Isaiah 30:15). The secret of health, wealth and outstanding achievement is in developing what is called the "quiet mind." By taking certain constructive words from the Bible, which represent the eternal truths of God and His Law, your mind becomes anchored on the Supreme Presence, which responds as you call upon It, and you experience the riches of the quiet mind.

2. Carlyle said: "Silence is the element in which great things fashion themselves." Emerson said: "Let us be silent that we may hear the whispers of the gods." Silently affirm that God is guiding you, that the

Divine wisdom will govern all your activities of the day, and that God thinks, speaks and acts through you every day. Claim Divine right action in all your undertakings. Practice transcendental meditation by imagining God's river of peace and love flowing through your whole being. As you do this, you will receive answers to all your problems welling up from the depths of yourself, and wonders will happen in your life. One man who practices this procedure has already received ideas worth over $200,000 for his corporation.

3. When you quiet your mind and immobilize your attention, realize only God knows the answer. Contemplate the answer, the solution, knowing that before you call, the answer is known to your Higher Self. You will discover there are creative answers in your subconscious that will revolutionize your life. One woman, during our silent period on Sunday morning, had a subliminal thought from her subconscious mind, which revealed to her that the man she was about to marry was already married and had two children.

4. *When he giveth quietness, who then can make trouble?* (Job 34:29). The suggestions, statements and actions of others cannot hurt you. The creative power is in you — it is the movement of your own thought. Does another person's thought govern you, or do you govern your own mind? When your thoughts are God's thoughts, God's power is with your thoughts of good.

5. If you have difficulty sleeping, talk to your body, telling it to relax, let go. Your body will obey you, and then affirm slowly and quietly, "I sleep in peace and I wake in joy, for He careth for me."

6. You can eradicate excess tension and anxiety by affirming the following spiritual truths three or four times daily: *Thou wilt keep him in perfect*

peace, whose mind is stayed on thee: because he trusteth in thee (Isaiah 26:3). *In quietness and confidence shall be your strength* (Isaiah 30:15). *Acquaint now thyself with him, and be at peace: thereby good shall come unto thee* (Job 22:21). *When he giveth quietness, who then can make trouble?* (Job 34:29). As you dwell on these great Biblical truths, a healing, therapeutic vibration permeates your entire body, and these spiritual vibrations enter into your subconscious mind neutralizing all the fear and worry patterns, and a sense of peace and tranquility will govern you.

7. A man's life is dyed by the color of his imagination. A salesman whose sales were dropping imagined his sales manager congratulating him on his excellent sales. He made a habit of running this mental movie twice a day, feeling the naturalness of the sales manager's handshake, hearing his voice, and lulling himself to sleep every night with the imaginary words of his sales manager: "Congratulations on your splendid success." By repetition he implanted the idea of promotion in his subconscious mind, and eventually he experienced a wonderful promotion and increase in salary.

8. The only place competition takes place is in your own mind; the idea of success and the thought of failure compete. You were born to succeed, not to fail. The Infinite within you can't fail. Give your attention to the idea of success and all the powers of your deeper mind will back you up. A sales manager was envious of a former classmate, and he did not know that this attitude of mind was causing his anxiety neurosis and interfering with his expansion. The remedy was simple. He decided to bless and prosper his former classmate, wishing for him all the blessings of life, and as he continued blessing him, all the envious and jealous thoughts lost mo-

mentum and his anxiety neurosis disappeared. Moreover, he was promoted to executive vice-president. By blessing the man whose promotion and success had previously annoyed him, he discovered he prospered himself also. Prayer always prospers.

9. A medical student was fearful and apprehensive about his examinations. Actually, he was fearing failure. This develops stress, which blocks the mind. He affirmed prior to sleep: "I am relaxed, at peace, poised, serene and calm. I have a perfect memory for everything I need to know at all times everywhere. I pass all examinations in Divine order. I sleep in peace and I wake in joy." These truths sank into his subconscious mind and he is now doing splendidly. He discovered the riches of the truth: *In quietness and confidence shall be your strength* (Isaiah 30:15).

10. You can get to experience the benefits of quieting the mind through using the meditation at the end of the chapter.

nineteen

How to Start
Living Like a King –
Almost Overnight

The Bible says: *I am come that they might have life, and that they might have it more abundantly* (John 10:10). Johann Goethe said: "Life is a quarry, out of which we are to mold and chisel and complete a character."

You are here to lead a full, joyous, successful and rich life along all lines. You were born to win, to conquer and to triumph over all obstacles. You are here to release your wonderful hidden talents, to bless mankind, and to express yourself at the highest possible level. Call upon Infinite Intelligence within you to reveal to you your true place in life and follow the lead which comes clearly and distinctly into your conscious, reasoning mind. When you find your true expression in life, you will be perfectly happy, and health, wealth, and all the other blessings of life will follow.

Your success and prosperity in the art of living a wonderful and glorious life depend on your habitual thinking and your heart's desire to transform your life from top to bottom. Remember, you go where your vision is, and your vision is that about which you are thinking, that where you are directing your attention, and the object where you are presently focused. Whatever you give attention to, your subconscious will magnify and multiply exceedingly in your life.

How a Woman Discovered $45,000 She Thought Lost

While writing this chapter, I was interrupted by a long distance telephone call from a woman in New York City, informing me that she had followed my advice and that her subconscious had revealed to her where the money was hidden.

Some months ago, her husband, who gambled considerably, had passed on. Prior to his passing, he had informed her that he was placing his winnings, $45,000, on the races for that day, in his desk drawer where it would be safe. Following his demise she unlocked the desk and looked through every drawer and examined all the papers and correspondence, but to no avail.

On the occasion of her first phone call, I suggested that she relax, let go completely, immobilize her attention, and just prior to sleep, to turn her request over to her subconscious mind as follows: "Infinite Intelligence in my subconscious knows exactly where the $45,000 is secreted and it is revealed to me now. I give thanks for the answer now."

On the third night following the above technique, her husband appeared to her in a dream and showed her exactly where the secret drawer was located and how, by pressing a certain button, it would open. She awakened immediately and found that the instructions were absolutely correct. To her joy and satisfaction, there was the $45,000 in twenty dollar bills neatly stacked away.

The psychic appearance of her husband in the dream was simply a dramatization of her subconscious mind, knowing that she would immediately follow instructions given and not think it was just an idle dream. The riches of your subconscious are indeed infinite in its manner of expression.

Hidden Riches Revealed by Meditation

A young man came to see me some months ago and said, "I'm a misfit. I'm a square peg in a round hole. I feel rejected and unwanted." I explained to him that the infinite storehouse of riches was in his subconscious mind and that he, like anybody else, could learn to tap it and bring forth all the wisdom, power and creative ideas he needed. Furthermore, I pointed out to him that each person is unique and that there is no misfit in a universe ruled by law and order; that no two people are alike any more than are two leaves of a tree or two crystals of snow. The Infinite never repeats Itself, as infinite differentiation is the law of life and there is no such thing as an unwanted man or woman. Emerson said: "I am an organ of God and God hath need of me where I am, otherwise I would not be here."

This simple explanation appealed to this young man, and he decided to apply the following simple prayer technique: "Infinite Intelligence reveals to me my hidden talents and shows me the way I should go. I know Infinite Intelligence is seeking expression through me and I follow the lead which comes to me. I am a focal point of Infinite Life in the same way that an electric bulb is a focal point for the manifestation of electricity. Infinite Life flows through me as harmony, health, peace, joy, growth and expansion along all lines. I give thanks for the answer which is mine now."

After a few days he felt a deep desire to take up public speaking and a course in applied salesmanship. Following a few months' training, he obtained a position as a representative for a manufacturer and has proven to be an excellent salesman and an asset to his organization.

Accept Wealth and Happiness Now

Now is the time. I talk to many people who are continuously looking forward to better times. Many are saying that some day they will be happy, prosperous and successful. Some are waiting for their children to grow up and get married; then they say they would travel to Europe and Asia and see the many strange, faraway places. A small percentage of the people I meet and converse with are waiting for the old folks to die; then they claim they would decide what to do.

All these people were waiting for something to happen, instead of realizing that God is the Eternal Now — their good is now, this moment, waiting for them to claim it. As you have seen demonstrated in this book by now, you are in command *now* for a full prosperous life.

One man said that someday he would hit the jackpot and make his mark on the world. His wife said that she hoped someday she would get a healing of her skin rash. I explained to both of them that all the powers of God were within each one of them. Peace is now. You can claim God's river of peace flows through you now. The Infinite Healing Presence is available and you can claim that this Healing Presence is flowing through you now, making you whole, pure and perfect.

It dawned on the husband and wife that wealth and healing are available now. This man's wife began to affirm night and morning as follows: "God's Healing Presence is saturating my whole being and Divine Love flows through my whole being. My skin is an envelope of God's love and is whole, pure and perfect without spot or blemish."

Within one week she proved to herself that the Infinite Healing was instantly available to her, and she had a complete healing.

I explained to her husband that wealth is available now, that it is a thought-image in the mind. He began to affirm boldly: "God's wealth is now circulating in my life. I am engraving this idea in my subconscious mind, and I know that whatever I impress on my subconscious mind will come to pass. I realize as I continue to do this that the response from my subconscious mind will be compulsive and I will be compelled to express wealth."

As he continued praying in the above manner, new creative ideas welled up within him. He made very large investments in gold stocks, both foreign and domestic, and in a matter of months he had earned a small fortune. He had a preponderant feeling, a sort of persistent intuitive urge to buy these stocks, all of which soared greatly in value immediately. He proved to himself that wealth was available here and now.

Claim Your Spiritual, Mental and Material Riches Now

Strength is *now*. Call on the Infinite Power of God within you and this power will respond, energizing, vitalizing and renewing your whole being now. Love is now. Claim that God's love envelops and saturates your mind and body. Realize and know that Divine Love is being filtered through you and manifested in all phases of your life. Guidance is now. Infinite Intelligence responds to your call. It knows only the answer and will reveal it to you now. Claim your good now. *You do not create anything;* all you do is to give form and expression to that which always was, now is, and ever shall be.

Moses and Jesus could have used a loud-speaker, a radio or a television. The idea or principle by which these are made always existed in the mind of the Infinite. When Plato referred to the "archetypes of Divine Mind," he referred to the fact that there is an idea or a pattern in Divine Mind behind every created thing in the universe.

Plan for a Rich Future Now

Remember that if you are planning something in the future, you are planning it now. If you are worried about the future, you are fearing it now. For example, if you are dwelling on the past, you are thinking of it now. You have control over your present thoughts. All you have to change are your present thoughts and keep them changed. You are aware of your present thoughts and all that you can realize is the outer manifestation of your habitual thinking at the present moment.

Beware of the Two Thieves Stealing from You

The "past" and the "future" are the two arch-thieves. If you are indulging in remorse and self-criticism over the past mistakes and hurts, the mental agony you experience is the pain of your present thought. If you are fearful about the future, you are robbing and stealing from yourself joy, health, happiness and peace of mind. Begin to count your blessings now and get rid of the two thieves.

To think of a happy and joyful episode in the past is a present joy. Remember, the results of past events — good or bad — are but the representation of your present thinking. Direct your present thoughts into the right channels. Enthrone in your mind peace, harmony, joy, love, prosperity and good will. Dwell consciously and frequently on these concepts and claim them and forget all other things.

Finally, brethren, whatsoever things are true, whatsoever things are honest, whatsoever things are just, whatsoever things are pure, whatsoever things are lovely, whatsoever things are of good report; if there be any virtue, and if there be any praise, think on these things (Philippians 4:8).

Take this spiritual medicine regularly and systematically and you will build a glorious future.

The Maid Thinks Big and Gets What She Wants

I am writing this chapter in Honolulu. I had a most interesting conversation with the Hawaiian maid who attends to my room in the Surfrider Hotel on the beach. I gave her some books to read, and she told me that some months previously a guest at the hotel had given her *Your Infinite Power to Be Rich,*[1] which she read avidly, applying the techniques for amassing riches outlined therein.

She added that after perusing the book, she began to think "big" and she made out an affirmation for herself: "I now possess and own a lovely car, which is a Divine idea in Divine Mind. I am driving it to and from my work every day It is fully paid for and I accept it now in my mind."

The sequel to her frequent affirmation and her joyous

---

[1]*Your Infinite Power to Be Rich* by Joseph Murphy, Parker Puolishing Company, Inc., West Nyack, New York, 1966.

expectancy of results was that she casually mentioned to one of the guests that she was praying for a car. This guest was a multi-millionaire and he casually said to her, "You can have my car. I'm buying a new one today." His car was a Cadillac, two years old and in excellent condition.

She said, "I got exactly what I prayed for. It was a complete gift with no strings attached, and now I am praying that Infinite Intelligence will attract to me a man who harmonizes with me perfectly. I know that will happen, too." Undoubtedly, she will get the answer she wants because she is thinking "big," and also because she understands that before she calls, the answer is already known in her subconscious mind.

How a Promotion and a Wonderful Increase in Salary Were Obtained

A junior executive once told me that he was trying hard for a promotion, but he added, "Others are ahead of me," "I'll have to wait," "I don't have priority," and so on. I told him frankly that he promoted himself; first, he would have to remove the barricade and stumbling blocks which were present in his own mind, such as his belief that he would have to wait perhaps for several years.

He decided to impregnate his subconscious mind with the idea of promotion, paying no attention to circumstances or conditions or the time element and looking to no one for promotion, but giving all his allegiance, loyalty and devotion to the Infinite Intelligence within him. Accordingly, he affirmed slowly, quietly, and feelingly several times a day as follows: "Promotion is mine now. Financial increase is mine now. Outstanding success is mine now. These ideas sink into my subconscious mind and I know that my deeper mind will compel me to express them."

In a few weeks' time he suddenly realized his cherished goal with an increase in prestige and a wonderful increase in salary.

How a Widow Discovered the Riches
Hidden in Her Mind

I recently interviewed a widow who said she had been praying four years for a husband but that she had never met the right man. In talking with her, I discovered she had been constantly postponing her good by such statements as, "I would like to marry when I retire; then I could travel to different parts of the world and be free to enjoy life with my husband," "I never meet the right men," and so on.

This widow had been projecting marriage in the future and was defeating her own purpose. She was unconsciously placing obstacles and delays in her own mind. I explained to her that she should always pray in the *now* and showed her how to collapse time by realizing first of all that before we experience anything, we must first claim it in our mind. I further explained that she marries character, or an ideal in her mind.

Accordingly, she prayed frequently as follows: "I am happily married now to a wonderful spiritual-minded man who harmonizes with me perfectly. There are mutual love, freedom and respect between us. I accept this man now, this moment, in my mind, and I know that the deeper currents of my mind bring both of us together in Divine order."

She practiced this prayer every night for a week, entering into the feeling and the delight that would be hers if she were already married. At the end of that time one of the teachers in the school proposed to her and I later had the privilege of performing the marriage ceremony. She proved to herself that you can realize the desire of your heart without procrastination. Her subconscious mind was the invisible matrimonial agent.

How He Secured Riches and Promotion

Recently a man visited me and during our conference elaborated on his many reverses. He concluded by blaming God for "punishing" him with bad luck, etc. I explained to him, however, that the universe is always one of law and order and that God, among other things, is a universal principle or law. If a man breaks a law, he will suffer accordingly. It is not a question of punishment by an angry God. On the contrary, it is an impersonal matter of cause and effect. If a man misuses the law of mind, for example, the reaction will be negative, but if he uses the law correctly it will help, heal and prosper him along all lines.

I instructed him how to become a free-flowing channel for Divine Life and gave him the following prayer meditation process to use frequently: "I am a clear, open channel of the Divine, and Infinite Life flows freely and joyously through me as health, peace, abundance, security and right action. I promote all my products in Divine order and I am constantly releasing new, creative ideas. I am constantly expanding spiritually, mentally and financially and am releasing the imprisoned splendor within."

This man has received two promotions in the past six months and has told me that the corporation with which he is associated has offered him the office of executive vice-president. He added joyfully, "I stopped blocking my good. I have taken my foot off the hose in a manner of speaking, and the waters of Life are flowing freely into my life."

This man has learned to tap the riches of the Infinite. Moreover, he has ceased pressing the weight of his negative mentality upon the pipeline of life. Shakespeare said, "All things be ready if the mind be so." So may it be with you!

MEDITATION FOR MIRACLE POWER STEPS TO RICHER LIVING AND FINANCIAL SUCCESS

It will pay you great dividends to use this meditation as often as possible:

"'Wist ye not that I be about my Father's business.' I know that my business, profession or activity is God's business. God's business is always basically successful. I am growing in wisdom and understanding every day. I know, believe and accept the fact that God's law of abundance is always working for me, through me and all around me.

"My business or profession is full of right action and right expression. The ideas, money, merchandise and contacts that I need are mine now and at all times. All these things are irresistibly attracted to me by the law of universal attraction. God is the life of my business; I am Divinely guided and inspired in all ways. Every day I am presented with wonderful opportunities to grow, expand and progress. I am building up goodwill. I am a great success, because I do business with others, as I would have them do it with me."

CHAPTER POINTS TO REMEMBER

1. You are here to lead the abundant life, a life full of love, peace, joy and rich living. Begin now to release the riches of the treasure house within you.

2. You go where your vision is. Whatever you give attention to, your subconscious will magnify and multiply in your experience.

3. The intelligence in your subconscious knows the answer to all problems. A woman wanted to know where $45,000 was secreted in her house by her late husband. She turned the request over to her subconscious prior to sleep and her deeper mind showed her exactly where the money was.

4. There is no such thing as an unwanted person in a universe ruled by law and order. Each person is unique and is born with different endowments. Claim that you are an organ of God and that God hath need of you where you are; otherwise, you would not be here. Realize that Infinite Intelligence is guiding you to your true expression and you will move onward and upward.

5. Accept your wealth, health and success now. Stop procrastinating. God is the Eternal Now! This means your good is now. Claim peace now. Claim that

God's Love fills your soul now, this minute. Wealth is a thought-image in your mind. Claim that God's wealth is circulating in your life now. As you make a habit of this, your subconscious will compel you to express wealth.

6. Claim all your good now. Remember, you do not really create anything; all you do is to give form and expression to that which always was, now is, and ever shall be. Moses and Jesus could have used radio, television and all our modern communication methods. The idea or principle behind all discoveries always existed in the mind of the Infinite.

7. Plan a rich and glorious future now. If you are planning something in the future, you are planning it now. If you are thinking about the past, you are thinking about it now. You can control the present moment. Change your present thought pattern to conform to health, wealth and success and your future is certain. Your future is your present thought pattern made manifest.

8. Beware of the two thieves. If you are indulging in remorse over past mistakes or are worrying about the future, you should be aware that these are the two thieves that rob you of vitality, discernment and peace of mind.

9. Think "big" and you will experience great things. A maid affirmed boldly, "I now possess and own a lovely car, which is a Divine idea, and I am driving it to and from my work. It is fully paid for and I accept it now." She received a gift of a wonderful car. This is the way her subconscious responded.

10. Never say to yourself, "I must wait years for promotion or an increase in salary." Never procrastinate, as that blocks your good. You pray in the Now always. Your subconscious takes you literally, and

when you say, "I'll have to wait," you are blocking your own good. Claim promotion and wealth now.

11. When you wish to marry, never say, "I would like to marry when I retire." You are projecting marriage into the future and are defeating your own purpose. Claim, "I am happily married now to a wonderful man who harmonizes with me perfectly," and your subconscious will respond accordingly.

12. God, or the Life Principle, never punishes. Man punishes himself by misuse of the law of his mind. Think good and good follows. Think negatively and negation follows. Use the following prayer frequently: "I am a clear, open channel of the Divine and Infinite Life which flows freely through me as harmony, health, peace, joy, abundance and security." Remember, it is as easy for God to become all these things in your life as it is to become a blade of grass. Become open and receptive to your good and you will discover that "All things be ready if the mind be so" (Shakespeare).

13. Use the meditation at the end of the chapter as your faultless guide in taking the miracle power steps to richer living and financial success.

twenty

The Lifetime Plan
for Infinite Riches

The Quiet Mind

God dwells at the center of my being. God is Peace: this Peace enfolds me in Its Arms now. There is a deep feeling of security, vitality, and strength underlying this peace. This inner sense of peace, in which I now dwell, is the Silent Brooding Presence of God. The Love and the Light of God watch over me, as a loving mother watches over the sleeping child. Deep in my heart is the Holy Presence that is my peace, my strength, and my source of supply.

All fear has vanished. I see God in all people; I see God manifest in all things. I am an instrument of the Divine Presence. I now release this inner peace; it flows through my entire being releasing and dissolving all problems; this is the peace that passeth understanding.

For Mental Poise

Whither shall I go from thy Spirit? Or whither shall I flee from thy Presence? If I ascend up into heaven, thou art there: if I make my bed in hell, behold, thou art there.

If I take the wings of the morning, and dwell in the uttermost parts of the sea, even there shall thy hand lead me, and thy right hand shall hold me." I am now full of a Divine enthusiasm because I am in the Presence of Divinity. I am in the Presence of All Power, Wisdom, Majesty, and Love.

The Light of God illumines my intellect; my mind is full of poise, balance, and equilibrium. There is a perfect mental adjustment to all things. I am at peace with my own thoughts. I rejoice in my work; it gives me joy and happiness. I draw continually upon my Divine Storehouse for It is the only Presence and the only Power. My mind is God's mind; I am at peace.

For Peace and Harmony in Daily Living

All is peace and harmony in my world, for God in me is "the Lord of Peace." I am the consciousness of God in action; I am always at peace. My mind is poised, serene, and calm. In this atmosphere of peace and goodwill which surrounds me, I feel a deep abiding strength and freedom from all fear. I now sense and feel the love and beauty of His Holy Presence. Day by day I am more aware of God's Love; all that is false falls away. I see God personified in all people. I know that as I allow this inner peace to flow through my being, all problems are solved. I dwell in God; therefore, I rest in the eternal arms of peace. My life is the life of God. My peace is the deep, unchanging peace of God; "It is the peace of God, which passeth all understanding."

For Controlling My Emotions

When a negative thought of fear, jealousy, or resentment enters my mind, I supplant it with the thought of God. My thoughts are God's thoughts, and God's Power is with my thoughts of good. I know I have complete dominion over my thoughts and emotions. I am a channel of the Divine. I now redirect all my feelings and emotions along harmonious, constructive lines. "The sons of God shouted for joy." I now rejoice to accept the ideas of God which are peace, harmony, and goodwill and I delight to express them; this heals all discord within me. Only God's ideas enter my mind, bringing me harmony, health, and peace.

God is Love. Perfect Love casteth out fear, resentment, and all negative states. I now fall in love with truth. I wish for all men everything I wish for myself; I radiate love, peace, and goodwill to all. I am at peace.

For Overcoming Fears of All Kinds

There is no fear, as "perfect Love casteth out fear." Today I permit Love to keep me in perfect harmony and peace with all levels of my world. My thoughts are loving, kind, and harmonious. I sense my oneness with God, for "in Him I live, move, and have my being."

I know that all my desires will be realized in perfect order. I trust the Divine Law within me to bring my ideals to pass. "The Father doeth the works." I am divine, spiritual, joyous, and absolutely fearless. I am now surrounded by the perfect peace of God; it is "the peace of God which passeth all understanding." I now place all my attention on the thing desired. I love this desire and I give it my whole-hearted attention.

My spirit is lifted into the mood of confidence and peace; this is the spirit of God moving in me. It gives me a sense of peace, security, and rest. Truly, "perfect Love casteth out fear."

For Overcoming Irritations in Any Circumstances

"He that is slow to wrath, is of great understanding; but he that is hasty of spirit exalteth folly." I am always poised, serene, and calm. The peace of God floods my mind and my whole being. I practice the Golden Rule and sincerely wish peace and goodwill to all men.

I know that the love of all things which are good penetrates my mind casting out all fear. I am now living in the joyous expectancy of the best. My mind is free from all worry and doubt. My words of truth now dissolve every negative thought and emotion within me. I forgive everyone; I open the doorway of my heart to God's Presence. My whole being is flooded with the light and understanding from within.

The petty things of life no longer irritate me. When fear, worry, and doubt knock at my door, faith in goodness, truth, and beauty opens the door, and there is no one there. O, God, thou art my God, and there is none else.

For Finding Serenity Under Any Condition

"He that dwelleth in the secret place of the most High shall abide under the shadow of the Almighty."

I dwell in the secret place of the most High; this is my own mind. All the thoughts entertained by me conform to harmony, peace, and goodwill. My mind is the dwelling place of happiness, joy, and a deep sense of security. All the thoughts that enter my mind contribute to my joy, peace, and general welfare. I live, move, and have my being in the atmosphere of good fellowship, love, and unity.

All the people that dwell in my mind are God's children. I am at peace in my mind with all the members of my household and all mankind. The same good I wish for myself, I wish for all men. I am living in the house of God now. I claim peace and happiness, for I know I dwell in the house of the Lord forever.

For Achieving the Balanced Mind for Wise and Intelligent Decisions

"Thou wilt keep him in perfect peace whose mind is stayed on thee, because he trusteth in thee." I know that the inner desires of my heart come from God within me. God wants me to be happy. The will of God for me is life, love, truth, and beauty. I mentally accept my good now and I become a perfect channel for the Divine.

I come into His Presence singing; I enter into His courts with praise; I am joyful and happy; I am still and poised.

The Still Small Voice whispers in my ear revealing to me my perfect answer. I am an expression of God. I am always in my true placè doing the thing I love to do. I refuse to accept the opinions of man as truth. I now turn within and I sense and feel the rhythm of the Divine. I hear the melody of God whispering its message of love to me.

My mind is God's mind, and I am always reflecting Divine wisdom and Divine intelligence. My brain symbolizes my capacity to think wisely and spiritually. God's ideas unfold within my mind with perfect sequence. I am always poised, balanced, serene, and calm, for I know that God will always reveal to me the perfect solution to all my needs.

For Achieving Victories Over All Obstacles to Richer Living

I now let go of everything; I enter into the realization of peace, harmony, and joy. God is all, over all, through all, and all in all. I lead the triumphant life, because I know that Divine Love guides, directs, sustains, and heals me. The Immaculate Presence of God is at the very center of my being; It is made manifest now in every atom of my body. There can be no delay, impediment, or obstruction to the realization of my heart's desire. The Almighty Power of God is now moving in my behalf. "None shall stay its hand, and say unto it, 'What doest thou?'" I know what I want; my desire is clear-cut and definite. I accept it completely in my mind. I remain faithful to the end. I have entered into the silent inner knowing that my prayer is answered and my mind is at peace.